WHAT ARE THEY SAYING ABOUT
THE PASTORAL EPISTLES?

What Are They Saying About the Pastoral Epistles?

Mark Harding

PAULIST PRESS
New York/Mahwah, N.J.

Library of Congress Cataloging-in-Publication Data

Harding, Mark.
    What are they saying about the Pastoral epistles / by Mark Harding.
       p. cm.
    Includes bibliographical references and index.
    ISBN 0-8091-3975-8
    1. Bible. N.T. Pastoral epistles—Criticism, interpretation, etc. I. Title.

BS2735.2 .H375 2000
227'.8306—dc21

00-049175

Distributed in Australia by
Rainbow Book Agencies Pty.Ltd/
Word of Life Distributors
303 Arthur Street
Fairfield, VIC 3078

Published by Paulist Press
997 Macarthur Boulevard
Mahwah, New Jersey 07430

www. paulistpress.com

Printed and bound in the
United States of America

Contents

To the clergy and people of
All Saints, Princeton

"I was hungry and you fed me."

Abbreviations

AnBib	Analecta biblica
ANF	Roberts, A., and J. Donaldson, eds. 1986 reprint. *The Ante-Nicene Fathers.* Ten volumes. Grand Rapids: Eerdmans.
ANRW	*Aufstieg und Niedergang der römischen Welt*
Apoc. Abr.	*Apocalypse of Abraham*
ATR	*Anglican Theological Review*
AusBR	*Australian Biblical Review*
BBR	*Bulletin for Biblical Research*
BJRL	*Bulletin of the John Rylands University Library of Manchester*
CBQ	*Catholic Biblical Quarterly*
1 Clem.	*1 Clement*
Clem. *Strom.*	Clement of Alexandria, *Stromateis*
Diogn.	*Epistle to Diognetus*

EKKNT	Evangelisch-katholischer Kommentar zum Neuen Testament
Exp	*Expositor*
ExpTim	*Expository Times*
FRLANT	Forschungen zur Religion und Literatur des Alten und Neuen Testaments
HTKNT	Herders theologischer Kommentar zum Neuen Testament
HTR	*Harvard Theological Review*
HUT	Hermeneutische Untersuchungen zur Theologie
Ign. *Eph.*	Ignatius, *Letter to the Ephesians*
Ign. *Pol.*	Ignatius, *Letter to Polycarp*
Ign. *Smyrn.*	Ignatius, *Letter to the Smyrnaeans*
JAAR	*Journal of the American Academy of Religion*
JAC	Jahrbuch für Antike und Christentum
JBL	*Journal of Biblical Literature*
JR	*Journal of Religion*
JRelS	*Journal of Religious Studies*
JRH	*Journal of Religious History*
JSNT	*Journal for the Study of the New Testament*
JSNTSup	Journal for the Study of the New Testament— Supplement Series

JTS	*Journal of Theological Studies*
LCL	Loeb Classical Library
LTP	*Laval théologique et philosophique*
NovT	*Novum Testamentum*
NTS	*New Testament Studies*
Pol. *Phil.*	Polycarp, *Letter to the Philippians*
Prot. Jas.	*Protevangelium of James*
RB	*Revue biblique*
RTR	*Reformed Theological Review*
SBL	Society of Biblical Literature
SBLDS	Society of Biblical Literature Dissertation Series
SBLMS	Society of Biblical Literature Monograph Series
SNTSMS	Society for New Testament Studies Monograph Series
StudBL	Studies in Biblical Literature
T. Sim.	*Testament of Simeon*
T12P	*Testaments of the Twelve Patriarchs*
WUNT	Wissenschaftliche Untersuchungen zum Neuen Testament

Preface

The writing of this book was made possible by a generous study leave grant from the Board of Delegates of the Australian College of Theology. I would like to thank the delegates for their insistence that I take this opportunity to write and be refreshed in so doing.

Equally generous was the provision of Visiting Scholar status at Princeton Theological Seminary for the first half of 1999. The seminary context provided, among other benefits, access to the rich resources of Speer Library and to a lively community of supportive scholars both within the seminary and in the wider township. In the midst of their busy lives, Randy Nichols, Jan Perkins, Milind Sojwal, Victor Preller, Gregory Faulkner, Peter Brown, and others, many of them parishioners of All Saints' Episcopal Church, Princeton, were all generous in allowing me the time to share something of my vision of the Pastoral Epistles and the joy of making new discoveries.

Finally, this book could not have been written without the patience and loving indulgence of my family, especially my wife Sue.

Mark Harding

Introduction

There is no shortage of scholarly research on the Pastoral Epistles. Commentaries, monographs, and articles continue to appear apace on this collection of three brief, purportedly Pauline letters, first termed "pastoral" by Paul Anton in 1726 (Lock 1924:xiii; Harrison 1921:13–14; Spicq 1969:1.31). Much of this enterprise is concerned with perennial questions of the authorship of the letters and the elucidation of their occasion as well as their literary and theological integrity. Their relationship to the other letters of the Pauline corpus, especially the seven homologoumena (Romans, 1 and 2 Corinthians, Galatians, Philippians, 1 Thessalonians, and Philemon), remains the subject of ongoing scholarly endeavor. In addition, there is a growing interest in the social setting of these letters as literature to be interpreted, as of first priority, in the light of that background.

Summary of the Contents of the Book

Chapter 1 deals with the authorship of the Pastorals. Most scholars are persuaded that the letters are post-Pauline and pseudonymous, that is, they were written in Paul's name by an unknown author (to whom I will usually refer as the Pastor). The Pastor sought to consolidate the Pauline identity of communities at the risk of affirming a disjunctive and, in the

3

author's mind, heterodox interpretation of the legacy of the apostle that was potentially socially dislocating. Since writing in his own name would not command the attention of the addressees, the author wrote in Paul's name even if that meant deceiving the faithful.

Defenders of Pauline authorship raise important questions regarding the implications of classifying the Pastoral Epistles as pseudepigrapha. Adding their voice to scholars of the phenomenon of pseudonymity in the Classical, hellenistic, and Greco-Roman eras, the defenders remind their audience that the early fathers, in common with their Greek and Roman forebears and contemporaries, were contemptuous of works they had reason to believe were nothing but literary hoaxes. Defenders of Pauline authorship express the view that claiming the Pastorals as pseudonymous seriously undermines their authority and compromises their canonical status. God could not have inspired "fraudulent" scripture. Nevertheless, arguments against the Pauline authorship of the letters have proven difficult to counter (as even staunch defenders will acknowledge) and raise important issues regarding the theological integrity of the homologoumena if the Pastorals are genuine. Moreover, the deception involved in writing pseudonymously may be justified in the cause of defending the apostolic faith in the face of teaching considered subversive. The problem raised by the phenomenon for New Testament study, and the Pastorals in particular, is discussed at the conclusion of chapter one.

Over the course of the twentieth century there were scholars who were quite prepared to view the Pastorals as a lamentable "fall" from the theological insights of the historical Paul (e.g., Schulz 1976:100–109; Hanson 1982:51). His arresting grasp of the significance of the Christ event was now eclipsed. The author domesticated the Pauline heritage, conforming it to prevailing Greco-Roman cultural mores.

Chapter 2 surveys important contributions of the current generation of scholars who have argued that the Pastorals must be primarily understood as actualizations of Pauline tradition to meet the contingencies of third generation believers resident in churches confessing a Pauline heritage. Recently scholars have also turned their attention to tracing the unique contribution of these letters to our understanding of the development of early Christianity, especially in its Pauline guise. Furthermore, the rediscovery of the apocryphal Acts, especially the (mid-to-late second century) *Acts of Paul,* a document judged by some to evoke a trajectory of Pauline tradition actually polemicized by the Pastor, has opened up fruitful avenues of inquiry. Scholars contrast the social and ecclesial mandates articulated in the Pastorals with the tradition encapsulated not only in the Acts but in the Gnostic scriptures as well. The letters continue to play a significant part in the debate within the churches of the various Christian traditions concerning the role of women within the church and in the wider society. At other junctures the Pastorals articulate theological ideas that have little to do with Paul and either derive from identifiable early Christian sources or are creative formulations by the author.

Chapter 3 surveys scholarly investigation of the social setting of the Pastoral Epistles. In the last twenty years an important collection of monographs has appeared which seek to understand the letters as the fruit of a dialogical relationship between their Greco-Roman setting and the constraints of the Christian confession of the addressees. This enterprise has served to highlight the historical particularity of the letters and has illuminated the author's social presuppositions. Consequently, scholars underline the potency of the Pastorals as vehicles of social conservatism within the churches for whom they were written.

Chapter 4 surveys the contribution of scholars to elucidating the literary setting of the letters. The Pastorals are literate commendations in letter-form of the author's interpretation of the Pauline heritage. Indeed, an essential strategy of the author is to write letters that evoke the apostle Paul as psychagogue, or spiritual director, of the communities he founded. This chapter also presents the contribution of recent scholarship toward understanding the Pastorals within their Greco-Roman epistolary context as letters of moral exhortation. As such, the Pastorals participate in a venerable tradition of paraenetic discourse, which, in literary terms, was first articulated in the deposit associated with the fourth-century B.C.E. Athenian, Isocrates.

The recent renewal of interest in Greco-Roman rhetoric and the detection of the use of rhetorical strategies in the letters have also served to highlight them as powerful advocates of the author's vision of life in church and society. This aspect of the Pastorals is the focus of Chapter 5. Not only are they self-conscious epistolary embodiments and affirmations of the Pauline heritage, they are rhetorically literate and sophisticated. The recent resurgence of interest in Greco-Roman rhetoric among biblical scholars has led to fruitful analyses of early Christian literature from the rhetorical perspective. In the case of the Pastorals it can be shown that the author uses strategies commended in the rhetorical handbooks for the presentation of persuasive arguments to promote his vision of ecclesiastical life. As a corpus, the letters, 2 Timothy especially, constitute Paul's "testament," his definitive and "last word." This is an essential characteristic of the author's persuasive intent in seeking a renewed commitment from his audiences to their apostle's legacy.

Conclusion

The Pastoral Epistles, like other documents of the New Testament canon, were originally addressed to believers. As part of the church's scriptural deposit they must be taken seriously by faith communities as documents written "from faith to faith." Nevertheless, it must be acknowledged that their very particularity calls for a creative interpretive response from pastors and teachers professing to stand in continuity with the original addressees of the letters, lest the letters be reduced to the status of relics of the unusable past. The purpose of this book is to survey and analyze recent scholarship on the Pastorals and to delineate potentially useful trends in that scholarship for the actualization of the message of these letters. The contribution of scholars to an understanding of the contemporary significance of the Pastorals is the focus of Chapter 6, and forms the conclusion of the book.

1

The Authorship of the Pastoral Epistles

Early Attestation

There is little doubt that the apostolic fathers knew and used letters of Paul and may have been familiar with a corpus of his letters. Polycarp's *Letter to the Philippians* (chs. 1–12) 4.1 and 9.2 (ca. 120–135 C.E.) contains possible allusions to 1 Timothy 6:7, 10 and 2 Timothy 4:10.[1] However, the three Pastorals are first cited and unmistakably attested to only in the last quarter of the second century C.E. Writing ca. 180 C.E., Athenagoras and Theophilus both cite 1 Timothy 2:1–2 and allude to other passages in the letters. Their contemporary, Irenaeus, cites each of the letters, referring to Paul as their author for the first time in extant sources.

Whether Marcion (fl. ca. 140 C.E.) actually knew the Pastorals or not, Tertullian (ca. 200) writes that he intentionally excluded them from his canon. Tertullian surmises that Marcion rejected them on the spurious basis that Paul did not write to individuals.[2] Tertullian knew that Marcion accepted Philemon, a letter written to an individual, as genuine. In *Stromateis* 2.11 (ANF 2.359), Clement of Alexandria (ca. 200) reports that there were Gnostics who, perceiving that they were the targets of the polemic of 1 Timothy 6:20–21, rejected both letters to Timothy. Jerome writes that

Basilides and Marcion rejected Titus, but that Tatian, an early Christian ascetic (d. ca. 170 C.E.), rejected the letters to Timothy but did accept Titus. In its list of authoritative books, the Muratorian Canon (ca. 200) includes the three Pastorals in the Pauline corpus.

In its extant form the earliest manuscript of a collection of Pauline letters (Hebrews included), namely, P46 (ca. 200 C.E.), does not contain 2 Thessalonians, Philemon, and the three Pastorals. Scholars argue that it is unlikely that the scribe intended to include them since there would have been insufficient space (Kenyon 1936:ix–x; Metzger 1992:37–38; Hahneman 1992:115–16). Consequently, some have also argued that the Pastoral Epistles were not part of the Pauline canon at that time, or were only slowly gaining that recognition.[3] While many scholars have rightly drawn attention to the lateness of their appearance in early Christian literature when compared to the other ten letters of the Pauline corpus, the early fathers, beginning with Irenaeus, unfailingly acknowledge them as Pauline.

The Pastoral Epistles as Pseudepigrapha

In the early nineteenth century, scholars began to raise doubts about the Pauline authorship of the Pastoral Epistles. J. E. C. Schmidt (1804) and F. D. E. Schleiermacher (1807) both doubted the genuineness of 1 Timothy. In the third volume of his *Einleitung in das Neue Testament* published in Leipzig in 1812, J. G. Eichhorn set out an extensive treatment of the non-Pauline authorship of all three letters. He argued for their pseudonymity on the grounds that they present compatible stylistic traits that can be effectively contrasted with the idiosyncratic style of the other letters of the Pauline corpus. He also observed that there was no place for the situations and concerns presupposed in the Pastorals if the apostle was also engaged at the same time in the writing of the other letters of the corpus.

In 1835, Ferdinand Christian Baur published a monograph in which he argued that the author's purpose was to counter the

teaching and practice of Marcion, such as his promotion of asceticism (see 1 Tim 4:1–5; 5:23) and the emancipation of women
(see 1 Tim 2:9–15). Baur maintained that Marcion's lost work, the
Antitheses, is actually mentioned by name in 1 Timothy 6:20
("Avoid the profane chatter and contradictions [Gr.: *antitheseis*])
of what is falsely called knowledge"). The theory has attracted a
few adherents in the twentieth century, among them Hans von
Campenhausen (1963:197–252) and R. Joseph Hoffmann (1984),
who argue that Polycarp was the probable author of the letters,
Edgar J. Goodspeed (1937:185) and Fred D. Gealy (1955:359).
Indeed, Hoffmann argues that the Pastorals emerge from an Eph-
esian circle, which included Polycarp, that sought to meet and
deflect the challenge of Marcion's interpretation of Paul. However, most modern scholars have been unprepared to date the letters as late as Baur did or to identify Marcionism as the false
teaching targeted by the author.

In 1880, Heinrich J. Holtzmann published his *Die Pastoralbriefe kritisch und exegetisch untersucht,* a magisterial study of
the letters in the form of analysis (1880:1–282) and commentary
(1880:283–504). In the analysis he mounts a thorough case for
their pseudonymity, synthesizing the insights of scholars to that
date. Reduced to their essence, the arguments he, and many scholars since, have adduced for the pseudonymity of the letters can be
grouped in five broad categories.

Arguments for the Pseudonymity of the Pastoral Epistles

1. The vocabulary and style are not consonant with the
   undisputed letters of Paul. Instead, the letters are replete
   with words, phrases, and grammatical constructions not
   found in the New Testament, let alone the Pauline corpus. By the same token, there are words and word groups
   distinctive to Paul that are not found at all in the Pastorals. Holtzmann also found evidence in the letters for

the lack of particles common to the undisputed letters that are marks of the apostle's dialogical style. P. N. Harrison enhanced the strength of the linguistic argument, at least for English readers, in his influential book entitled *The Problem of the Pastoral Epistles* (1921). He counted 175 New Testament *hapax legomena* in the letters. Sixty-one appear in the apostolic fathers (ca. 95–145 C.E.) and the apologists (ca. 140–170 C.E.), while a further 32 appear in the apologists alone. The remaining 82 are not found in either corpus but in contemporary writers. Some of these 82 words are also found in earlier Greek writers (1921:161–64). Harrison concludes that the author of the Pastorals does not speak the language of Paul but rather speaks "the language of the Apostolic Fathers and Apologists" (1921:70). Harrison also lists phrases in the letters that are distinctly echoed in the early second-century writers (1921:165; 1955:79–80).

The examination of the style of the Pastorals with respect to the rest of the Pauline corpus to determine the authenticity of the letters has produced ambiguous results. Two recent monographs demonstrate that, though objective criteria are utilized in these studies, determination of what aspects of style are to be investigated and the assessments of the results are just as much indebted to subjectivity as any other discussion of the authenticity of the Pastorals. In his *A Stylometric Study of the New Testament* (1986), Anthony J. P. Kenny concludes that, with the exception of Titus, there is reason to maintain the view that the remaining 12 letters are the work of a single, versatile author. On the other hand, Kenneth J. Neumann draws contrasting conclusions in his *The Authenticity of the Pauline Epistles in the Light of Stylostatistical Analysis* (1990). Basing his research on a different set of criteria, he perceives substantial differences between the Pastorals and the rest of the Pauline corpus. Neumann agrees with a number of scholars that *hapax legomena* are an inadequate criterion for determining authorship.

The use of such words may be attributed to circumstantial or accidental differences (cf. Spicq 1969:1.193).[4] However, Harrison argued that the language of the author of the Pastorals has moved well beyond the cultural milieu of Paul.

2. The Pastorals lack the great themes and ideas of the Pauline correspondence. The Pastor does not speak of the cross or justification by faith. There is no mention of Paul's ecclesiologically foundational idea of the "body of Christ" or the concept of being "in Christ" in the sense of being in an intimate personal relationship with him. The expectation of the imminence of the parousia (1 Cor 7:29; Rom 13:11–14; 1 Thess 4:17; 1 Cor 15:51) is less urgent. Faith has become synonymous with the *regula fidei* or is ranked with the virtues, such as love, holiness, and modesty (1 Tim 2:15) or righteousness, godliness, endurance, and gentleness (1 Tim 6:11). Nor do we find the great salvation-historical themes of the Pauline correspondence, such as the priority of Israel or the role played by the Jewish law. The Pastorals have their own distinctive theological ethos.

3. The personal information included in the Pastoral Epistles finds no place in the career of Paul as we know it from the rest of the letters of the Pauline corpus, the Acts of the Apostles, or from independent historical sources. According to Romans 15:23–24, 28, Paul has completed his work in the east (compare Acts 20:25, 38) and is intending to visit Spain as the next theater of his work.[5] *1 Clement* 5.7 (ca. 95 C.E.) speaks of Paul having been martyred once he had reached "the limits of the west." Clement may have Rome, not Spain, in mind. If he did know a tradition that Paul reached Spain, he seems to know of only one imprisonment. On the other hand, the Pastorals seem to presuppose a release from the captivity reported at the end of Acts prior to renewed missionary

activity in the east. Accordingly, the letters have influenced later writers, such as Eusebius (*Ecclesiastical History* 2.22.2).

4. The teaching of the false teachers is not compatible with that of Paul's opponents in the undisputed letters. Assuming the Pastorals to be addressing real situations, the opponents appear to belong to a Jewish-Christian proto-Gnostic movement. They mandate asceticism with respect to marriage, food, and drink. They are concerned, inter alia, about "myths and genealogies" and teach a realized eschatology (Brox 1969:31–42; Towner 1987:95–124; Redalié 1994:376–97; Bassler 1996:25–31). They are countered not by reasoned argument as in the undisputed letters and Colossians but in the main by polemic and vilification (Brox 1969:39–41). Furthermore, the addressees are to "guard the deposit," to hold fast to the true teaching, and to continue to work for the maintaining and affirming (1 Timothy) or establishing (Titus) of structures that will protect the faithful from the inroads of false teachers in the present and the future.

5. The organization of the churches mandated in the Pastoral Epistles does not match the character of that encountered in the undisputed letters. In the latter the exercise of gifts of leadership, edification, and other mutually beneficial ministries are all inspired by the one Spirit (Rom 12:6; 1 Cor 12:4–11). However, the Pastor knows a spiritual endowment for congregational ministry (1 Tim 4:14; 2 Tim 1:6) restricted to males who exercise leadership (1 Tim 2:12; 3:2, 4; Titus 1:9). The ecclesiology of the letters has more in common with what is encountered in the Ignatian correspondence, ca. 110, than the house-churches of the Pauline mission. Ecclesiastical life has come to be centered on official ministers—the bishop, presbyters, and deacons. It would not be improper to perceive in the Pastorals the

beginnings of an ordained ministry and lay acceptance of and submission to that ministry.

The effect of these arguments is cumulative (Easton 1947:15). Discussion of authorship in, say, Jürgen Roloff's commentary on 1 Timothy (1988), Yann Redalié's *Paul après Paul* (1994), or Lorenz Oberlinner's recent three-volume commentary on the letters (1994–96), testifies to the persistence and persuasiveness of the case against Pauline authorship exhaustively outlined by Holtzmann. We can speak, however, of certain enhancements of this basic position.

J. Christiaan Beker

J. Christiaan Beker's *Heirs of Paul* (1991) examines the post-Paulines, the Pastoral Epistles included, from the perspective of his coherence/contingency model so fruitfully applied to the undisputed letters in his major study, *Paul the Apostle* (1980). Beker argues that the undisputed Pauline letters should be understood as dialogical communications in which the contingencies of those churches are engaged by what Beker terms the "coherent" structure of Paul's interpretation of the Christ event. The structure of Paul's thought has its origin in his preconversion apocalyptic worldview. That worldview was decisively affirmed in his encounter with the risen Christ. The undisputed letters are particular manifestations of a creative hermeneutic in which the apocalyptic structure of the apostle's thought is brought into dialogue with his audiences in a way that not only maintains the integrity of that thought but intelligibly addresses their contingent situations.

Beker argues that the Pastorals signal their non-Pauline authorship in two ways. The Pastor does not articulate Paul's apocalyptic interpretation of the significance of the Christ event. The parousia hope has receded. The Pastor wishes to ensure that his addressees live according to the moral conventions of the day. Gone is the radical expectation of an imminent end with Paul's far-reaching re-evaluation of what it means in the present to be "in Christ." Furthermore, the Pastor is not at all concerned to enter into dialogue with the false teachers. He prefers to engage in polemic and vilification from a distance. He issues decrees to his addressees, urging them to guard the "deposit" (1 Tim 6:20; 2 Tim 1:14)—veritably "frozen," to use Beker's apt term—and to choose those who will likewise protect it and pass it on to faithful successors (2 Tim 2:2). According to the Pastor, the Pauline heritage will alone secure the addressees in the faith that has been delivered to them and will ensure the salvation of those who submit to its prescriptions.

Counterproposals

Secretary Theories

Responses to arguments against Pauline authorship have taken several forms. A number of scholars contend that the pervasive and inescapable non-Pauline characteristics of the Pastoral Epistles, particularly those respecting their distinctive vocabulary and theology, are evidence of the work of a secretary writing at Paul's direction.[6] Some have nominated Luke as the actual author of the Pastorals. C. F. D. Moule (1965:430–52) and Stephen G. Wilson (1979) are two advocates of this hypothesis.

Moule confesses serious doubts about the Pauline authorship of the letters, drawing attention to their vocabulary and style, and more particularly to the decidedly un–Pauline caste of certain of their theological formulations, such as the passage concerning the proper use of the Jewish law in 1 Timothy 1:8–9. Here the author observes that the law was not intended for the "innocent" but as the means of restraining the lawless and disobedient. Paul, with his view of the law as the revelation of the demand of God for all, could not have written this. Yet, in order to account for the convincingly Pauline character of the personalia and the Pastorals' affinities with Lukan style and thought, Moule argues that

Luke wrote all three letters at Paul's request and before Paul's death (note 2 Tim 4:11).

Wilson argues that the letters were written by Luke after the completion of Acts, incorporating "travel notes" upon which he alighted in his travels collecting letters of Paul among the churches.[7] He surmises that Luke used these notes "as a peg on which to hang his pseudonymous letters" (1979:4). Wilson mounts a full-scale examination not only of certain affinities of vocabulary and style between Luke-Acts and the Pastorals but their similar ecclesiological and theological outlook. Eschatology, he contends, is "a visible but inconspicuous theme" in both (1979:18). The term *godliness* (Gr.: *eusebeia*), an esteemed religious ideal in hellenistic philosophy, occurs only in the Pastorals and Luke-Acts. Wilson observes that only Luke-Acts and the letters know of overseers (Gr.: *episkopoi*) and presbyters (see Acts 20:28). Both speak of the activity of prophets and refer to the office of evangelist. Paul's farewell speech in Acts 20:18–35 is markedly evocative of all three Pastorals. Luke-Acts echoes the Savior Christology of the letters. Luke's portrait of Paul also bears comparison with the image of Paul in the Pastorals.

However, there are difficulties with the Lukan hypothesis. Against Moule it might be argued that, unlike other letters of the Pauline corpus, the Pastorals give no evidence that a secretary was involved in their writing. Luke is reticent about calling Paul an apostle (only in Acts 14:4, 14, and then only in conjunction with Barnabas), preferring to restrict the term to the Twelve. Yet each of the openings of the Pastorals herald Paul as apostle (see also 1 Tim 2:7; 2 Tim 1:11). There is no sense in the letters that Paul shares apostolic status with others (contrast Gal 1–2; 1 Cor 15:9). While there are some theological and verbal affinities, these may be better explained in other ways. For example, Luke-Acts and the Pastorals are roughly contemporaneous writings, and their respective communities are both informed by similar Christian traditions and influenced by the same hellenistic milieu.

Finally, while the author seems to know other Pauline letters, this is doubtful for Luke.

Fragment Hypotheses

Other scholars have been persuaded that there are genuine Pauline fragments embedded within the otherwise pseudepigraphical letters. We have already considered the contribution of P. N. Harrison to the consolidation of arguments for the non-Pauline authorship of the Pastoral Epistles. In his *Problem of the Pastoral Epistles,* Harrison identified five "genuine notes." These are (1) Titus 3:12–15, (2) 2 Timothy 4:13–15, 20, 21a, (3) 2 Timothy 4:16–18a, (4) 2 Timothy 4:9–12, 22b, and (5) 2 Timothy 1:16–18; 3:10–11; 4:1–2a, 5b, 6–8, 18b, 19, 21b, and 22a. Here the non-Pauline characteristics recede. The personalia, which Harrison cannot accept as fiction, come to the fore as genuinely Pauline.

In *The Pastoral Letters as Composite Documents* (1997), James D. Miller advances the thesis that the letters are composite documents derived from disparate, preformed material, including genuine Pauline fragments. The lack of sustained argument and logical development of thought in the letters betrays their essential nature as loosely constructed archival anthologies. The result is that the letters read "like a Hellenistic moral handbook" (1997:113). In their present form, the Pastorals amount to the longer recension of a Pauline core. 1 Timothy, for example, was originally composed of 1:1–7, 18–20; 3:14–15; and 6:20–21. Titus 3:12–15 may represent the original core around which the rest of traditional material of the present letter to Titus was gathered. The Pastorals are not the work of a single author but emanate from a school of Pauline disciples committed to the training of pastors. The school was responsible for editing texts in a manner similar to the way in which many other ancient books and corpora reached their final form. The books of Jeremiah and Isaiah, many of the Dead Sea Scrolls, the *Didache,* Polycarp's *Letter to the Philippians,* and the *Epistle to Diognetus* all reached their final form, Miller contends, by an analogous method. In the case of our letters the process may have taken 100 years. The longer recension of the letters of Ignatius serves Miller as the best model for the crafting of the Pastoral Epistles.

The thrust of Miller's literary analysis of the letters will be revisited in Chapter 5. Few scholars will doubt that he is correct in his identification of certain preformed materials in the Pastorals, such as hymnic and credal statements. However, is there evidence that schools, such as the one responsible for the letters in their present form, obliterate the original textual core *(Grundlage)* so that it can only now be brought to light through a painstaking paring away of layers of preformed material? This is not what we actually encounter in the examples tendered by Miller. The longer recension of the original Ignatian letters is comprised of expansions of each paragraph of the original letters. Even though the resultant letters are about twice as long as the originals, the longer recension preserves the original content and thought flow. The original textual forms of the *Epistle to Diognetus* and *Polycarp's Letter to the Philippians* are quite clearly supplemented by appendices. The force and focus of the originals of these documents are not eclipsed by the additional and supplementary material, as is the case in Miller's thesis of the growth of the Pastorals from core to final form.

Defenders of Pauline Authorship

It would be a serious mistake to dismiss the research and concerns of the defenders of Pauline authorship. This is particularly so with respect to those who raise the problem of the occasion of the letters and the appropriateness of the presence of pseudepigrapha in the New Testament canon.

Although Ceslaus Spicq's two-volume commentary was first published in 1947 and last re-issued in a fourth edition in 1969, it remains the most extensive and cogent vindication of Pauline authorship, but by no means the only defense, produced in the last generation. Spicq observes that the Pastoral Epistles are largely different from the other letters of the Pauline corpus. Not only are they private communications to trusted individuals, they resemble the exhortatory treatises associated with Isocrates and the letters of Seneca to Lucilius (1969:1.38–39, 41–42). As such, the Pastorals form a unique collection within the Pauline corpus with respect to their subject matter and genre. The juxtaposition of diverse topics in the Pastorals suggest further comparisons with the contemporaneous exhortatory letters of Seneca to Lucilius (1969:1.41–42). But if the letters are not by Paul, that is, if they are pseudonymous, they do not belong in the canon.

Spicq contends that the false teachers polemicized in the letters, far from being second-century Gnostics, are Jewish-Christian proto-Gnostics such as those Paul also encountered earlier in his ministry in his dealings with the Corinthian church (1969:1.114; see 1 Cor 4:18–20; 2 Cor 10:4–5). While the letters cannot be fitted into the career of Paul as we know it from the New Testament, Spicq argues that Paul was released from the imprisonment of Acts 28 for further missionary enterprise in Spain to which *1 Clement* 5.7 testifies. His return to his eastern theater occurred thereafter, followed by arrest, a second trial, and execution in Rome in the last year or two of Nero's reign. Theological positions espoused in the Pastorals are consonant with those of the other letters of the corpus, though not always expressed in familiar language. Though the letters articulate a Christology not otherwise encountered in the Pauline corpus, Paul is seeking to counteract the claims of the imperial cult in which the Caesars are celebrated as embodiments of divine saving intervention (1969:1.251–54). The ecclesiology of the church and its hierarchical ordering is an entirely expected development, given Paul's apostolic oversight of his churches. That oversight is now being passed on to Timothy and Titus. Ecclesiastical officials are already found in the Pauline correspondence (see Phil 1:1) and Acts (see 14:23; 20:17, 28). Far from there being evidence of the cessation of charismata in the

Pastorals, the exercise of the gifts are to be closely monitored by Paul's successors just as he, as an apostle, exercised oversight in the churches he founded.

Paul must be allowed room to adapt his message to meet the needs of his addressees. Spicq reproaches Harrison for giving the impression in his *Problem of the Pastoral Epistles* (1921) that the *hapax legomena* of the letters are only attested to in second-century writers and that there are no first-century parallels. On the contrary, a significant proportion of these words are in fact found in the Septuagint,[8] as well as in Philo (d. ca. 40 C.E.), whom Paul may have read. In passing, Spicq does allow for the possibility that a secretary, perhaps Luke, might be responsible for some of the instances of alleged un-Pauline vocabulary and style of the letters (1969:1.199).

Spicq's discussion is significant for his view of the adaptability of the apostle in articulating his message in the light of the situation of his delegates and their churches. In the Pastorals, Paul is addressing a decidedly Gentile audience. The outbreak of the Jewish War (66–70 C.E.), Spicq surmises, sundered the church irrevocably from its Jewish origins (1969:1.294–5). The letters bear testimony to new directions for the Pauline churches in which the concerns of Gentiles are increasingly uppermost. Timothy (Acts 16:1, 3) and Titus (Gal 2:3) are well placed to mediate Paul's heritage to their Gentile Christian communities in language and concepts that are distinctively hellenistic. In the Pastoral Epistles, Paul's ethics are for the first time expressed in the language of virtue sanctioned by the philosophical tradition of the cultural milieu of the churches of his delegates (1969:1.175, 294).

Spicq contends that the letters capture the temper of an old man, one acutely aware of the need to bequeath his heritage to younger successors. Noting the frequency of formulaic phrases such as "the saying is sure," the solemnity of the doxologies and credal formulae, and the density of the doctrinal statements, Spicq concludes that Paul's thoughts and patterns of speech are all redolent of old age, even senescence, and the approach of death.[9]

Many will find it difficult to accept that Paul has ceased to be impelled by the defining issues of the other letters of the corpus. The disappearance of his earlier insistence on the centrality of the cross for understanding Christian existence, for example, is inexplicable, especially if Paul is concerned about his delegates guarding and passing on the "deposit," his heritage, to their successors. Spicq conceives of a Paul who simply has no need to continue articulating his earlier commitment to the priority of Israel, the role of the law, and Israel's place in the salvation-historical purposes of God, as though these were issues that ultimately were not essential to Paul's perception of the significance of the Christ event. He merely acquiesces in the sundering of the church from the Jewish cast of his gospel with its apocalyptic tenor and celebration of eschatological realities already in train in the church. The Paul of the undisputed letters would not, I believe, stand idly by while the church "moved on," as it were, into the mainstream of Gentile culture and social sensibility as though its Jewish heritage could be sloughed off.[10] Acts and the homologoumena agree that it was the highly symbolic and eschatologically charged collection of money from Gentile believers for the Jerusalem church that brought Paul and his entourage to Jerusalem at the end of the 50s C.E. (Acts 24:17; Rom 15:25–26; cf. 2 Cor 8:1–4, 19). The very reasons for Paul's arrest (see Acts 21) and the defining circumstances that eventually saw him insist on appearing before the emperor have, incredibly, ceased to matter to the Paul of the Pastorals. Less than a decade later the apostle has forgotten those things that indelibly stamped his apostleship and propelled him into the world of Jews and Gentiles to argue and debate in synagogues. There he busily proclaimed to both "nations" the news that in Christ God has confirmed his promises to the patriarchs. In Christ there is an end to the law, and the creation of a new people in Christ where once there was division and separation between Jew and Greek, male and female, and slave and free.

Recently several scholars have argued that 2 Timothy is, or might well be, a genuine letter of Paul. In his *Paul the Letter-*

Writer and the Second Letter to Timothy (1989) Michael Prior vigorously contends that the whole of the letter is genuine, and, incidentally, that the other Pastorals are genuine as well. Prior is persuaded that 2 Timothy is neither Paul's farewell before his execution nor his testament. This interpretation, he argues, has been foisted on the letter by commentators influenced by the tradition that his execution is imminent. Paul's talk of his "release" in 2 Timothy 4:6 refers not to his impending death (as the context, it seems to me, inescapably suggests), but to his release from imprisonment. Subsequently Paul will again take up his missionary brief, this time in Spain, a turn of events to which the Muratorian Canon and the *Acts of Peter* testify. Some of the differences between the Pastorals and the rest of the Pauline corpus can thus be explained on the ground that in the Pastorals we hear Paul himself speaking, writing in his own name without the mediation of secretaries and co-authors. This point is also seriously considered by Philip H. Towner, a recent defender of Pauline authorship, in his *1–2 Timothy & Titus* (1994:35). However, the thought that the apostle's authentic voice might be more faithfully articulated in the Pastorals than in the other letters of the Pauline corpus raises profound and, quite frankly, disturbing questions for the concept and location of the essence of Paul's thought.

Jerome Murphy-O'Connor builds on this thesis of Prior's in his article "2 Timothy Contrasted with 1 Timothy and Titus" (1991:403–18). Murphy-O'Connor detects 30 differences between 2 Timothy and 1 Timothy/Titus. In terms of 2 Timothy's Christological formulations, the delineation of the ecclesiastical bureaucracy, and description of the false teachers, he concludes that there is sufficient ground for positively ruling our common authorship. He stops short of nominating Paul as the author. Similarities between the later 1 Timothy and Titus are due to imitation of 2 Timothy on the part of their author. In his more recent *Paul the Letter-Writer: His World, His Options, His Skills* (1995), Murphy-O'Connor does speak of the "authenticity" of 2 Timothy. Nevertheless it is difficult to see how any of the differences he isolates necessarily rules out common authorship.

In *Letters to Paul's Delegates: 1 Timothy, 2 Timothy, Titus* (1996), Luke Timothy Johnson expresses the view that each of the letters, 2 Timothy especially, could have been written by Paul. While the letters cannot be fitted into the chronology of Paul's life as we know it, we must also confess that there are gaps in our knowledge of his career in which the situations alluded to in the letters could have occurred.[11] The style of the Pastorals evidences a mixture of Pauline and non-Pauline elements, the vocabulary of 2 Timothy being closer to the other Paulines. Yet no early Christian writer ever raised doubts about the authenticity of the Pastorals on this ground. Criteria of style were invoked by early fathers in considering the merits of attributing common authorship to 1 and 2 Peter (Jerome), Hebrews and the Pauline corpus (Origen), and Revelation and the Fourth Gospel (Dionysius of Alexandria). The structure of the church in the Pastorals is closer to that evidenced in the Pauline churches and the diaspora synagogue than, say, in Ignatius. The most difficult issue, Johnson acknowledges, is the theology of the letters. However, all of Paul's letters, Johnson concludes, are affected by contingencies such as the "subject matter, audience, traditions Paul employs, [and] literary conventions demanded by the circumstances" (1996:18). Nevertheless many scholars will remain unconvinced that the problem of the unprecedented particularity of the Pastorals over against the rest of the Pauline letters is adequately addressed in this fashion.

The Pastoral Epistles and the Problem of Pseudonymity

In his commentary, Luke Timothy Johnson challenges proponents of pseudonymous authorship to identify the situation(s) under which the letters came to be written and accepted as genuine. George W. Knight III issues a more strident challenge in *The Pastoral Epistles* (1992). Contenders for the pseudonymity of the

Pastorals, he proposes, have a responsibility to show cause why the surface claim of the letters should be set aside. Moreover, the fathers were capable of determining whether or not works had been penned pseudonymously. In similar fashion, E. Earle Ellis (1992:212–24) argues that unethical deception and pseudonymity go hand in hand. If the Pastorals are pseudonymous, they have been included in the canon unworthily and should be removed.[12] Stanley E. Porter voices similar concerns in a provocative article, "Pauline Authorship and the Pastoral Epistles: Implications for the Canon" (1995:105–23). After surveying arguments against the authenticity of the letters and recent significant scholarship on pseudonymity, he poses the following question. If the Pastorals are as clearly pseudonymous as most modern scholars maintain, how were they ever accepted into the canon? Since the fathers failed to detect their pseudonymous character, accepting only those works that had impeccable apostolic pedigrees and rejecting others that were pseudonymous, perhaps we should now exclude the Pastorals from the canon.[13]

In his *Falsche Verfasserangaben* (1975), Norbert Brox's discussion of the phenomenon of pseudonymity ranges over the Greco-Roman literary tradition, the Hebrew Bible, the literature of early Judaism, and the New Testament. He also surveys the encounter of the early fathers with the problem of pseudepigraphy. He senses that many pseudepigraphers were motivated to attribute their works to the ancients by the overwhelming sense of respect for the venerable past. He notes the practice of certain philosophical schools, notably the Pythagoreans, which disseminated and extended the teaching of their revered master by generating pseudepigrapha. He also observes that there was a highly developed sense of the lie told for a noble purpose, a concept discussed at length in Plato.[14] On this basis he argues that pseudepigrapha might be written in the name of another, a worthy from the distant or not so distant past, to address an urgent and critical need. Consequently, if there is deception in the writing of the Pastorals it is justified on the ground that writing pseudonymously presented a sure way to defend the Pauline heritage in the face of false teaching (cf. Metzger 1972:3–24).

Lewis Donelson argues similarly. The second century was a period in which competing and opposing understandings of the Christian life-commitment were vigorously and bitterly debated. His survey of second-century epistolary pseudepigrapha in chapter one of his monograph *Pseudepigrapha and Ethical Argument in the Pastoral Epistles* (1986:7–66) demonstrates how frequently the names of apostles and other great figures of the apostolic era were invoked as the authorities behind the views espoused in the extant documents. In the early church, writers looked to the apostolic era for guidance and vindication as they rose to meet the challenge of defending the faith against the teaching of "heretics." That meant writing in the name of an apostle, a contemporary, or associate at the risk of one's literary deception being uncovered. Yet no one, Donelson observes, "seems to have accepted a document as religiously and philosophically prescriptive which was known to have been forged" (1986:11, 16; McDonald 1995:232).[15] However, the maintenance of the apostolic faith in the church justified deceiving it because the need for the "good lie" was great (1986:20). But the task did require uncommon skill. If pseudepigraphers were going to succeed in their deception they had to create the illusion that their work was genuine. On this ground, the personalia of the Pastorals can be explained as bold strategies, by no means unprecedented in ancient literature, designed to enhance their aura of verisimilitude (1986:54–66). The writing of pseudepigrapha, then, was an essential part of the process by which early leaders—both "orthodox" and "heterodox"—sought to define and establish the boundaries of that faith. In the case of the Pastorals, Paul was being reclaimed for the "orthodox" offensive against the "heretics" (Donelson 1986:59–65; cf. Bauer 1971:226; Hoffmann 1984:282–87).

Finally, Donelson argues that there is an integral relationship between apostolic doctrine and apostolic authorship such that convictions that the content of a book accords with orthodox doctrine become determinative with respect to the attribution or the affirmation of apostolic authorship (1986:42–54, 55 n.186).[16] This is well illustrated in Tertullian and Eusebius. Both testify to the rejection of spurious documents, neither of them pseudepigrapha it must be acknowledged, primarily because of the doctrinal unorthodoxy they are discovered to contain.[17] The Pastorals, on the other hand, were regarded as genuine from the time they began to be cited as Pauline—that is, from Irenaeus on—because they were persuasive at the level of their teaching and their evocation of the character of the apostle. What the Pastorals affirmed was consistent with what the orthodox teachers confessed. Above all, as the frequency of citations in Irenaeus and Tertullian demonstrates, they were supremely useful in combating the Marcionite and Gnostic "heretics," for whom Paul was the apostle par excellence.

Conclusion

It is apparent that the debate concerning the authorship of the Pastorals has elicited, on the one hand, a set of powerful arguments for pseudonymous authorship and, on the other, a variety of counterproposals. Secretary and fragment hypotheses still command some support. Defenders of Pauline authorship contend that the integrity of the canon and the authority of scripture would be subverted by the presence of pseudepigrapha in the Bible.[18]

The challenges posed by the defenders have been taken up by recent scholars such as Lewis Donelson (1986). He understands the Pastorals as early second century attempts to legitimize the author's defense of the apostolic faith for the protection of churches faced by "heterodox" teaching and to rehabilitate the apostle among the "orthodox." However, he has little confidence that the author has understood the distinctive message of the apostle. The Pastor is defending, Donelson writes, "a man he knows mostly by reputation and legend" (1986:60). The question of the extent to which the author has brought Paul's message to speech is the subject of the chapter to follow.

2
The Pastoral Epistles and Pauline Tradition

Introduction

Proponents of the pseudonymity of the letters have argued that the theology articulated in them is largely incompatible with the theology of the Pauline corpus, especially the undisputed letters. Some scholars speak of the Pastorals as encapsulating a "jaded" Paulinism or a "fall" from Paul. For others, they are testimony to the emergence of "early Catholicism," the letters heralding the increasing institutionalization of the church and the replacement of charismatic endowments by the exercise of officially recognized ministries. On the other hand, defenders of Pauline authorship have argued that the distinctive theology expressed in the letters is contingent upon the unprecedented situation of the addressees. Issues that had earlier dominated Paul's correspondence with their Jewish-Christian focus are superseded by concerns more congenial to Gentiles unfamiliar with the original Jewish cast of his gospel.

Pauline Tradition in the Pastoral Epistles

Since the 1960s, a number of scholars have focused attention on the content of the Pauline tradition articulated in the letters. These scholars analyze the Pastorals as actualizations and embodiments of Pauline tradition. Several contemporary scholars, such as Norbert Brox (1969:67–68) and Jürgen Roloff (1988:39–40), believe that the author of the Pastorals knew and communicated the Pauline tradition that is found chiefly in the ten-letter Pauline corpus and to a lesser extent in the Acts of the Apostles (cf. Barnett 1941:277; Trummer 1978:88–89). In a careful analysis of the literary relationships between the Pastorals and the other canonical Pauline letters, Albert E. Barnett concluded that the Pastorals allude to every Pauline letter.[1] Brox is one of many scholars who trace the tradition brought to speech in the Pastorals to detail encountered in passages in Acts, especially Paul's farewell speech recorded in Acts 20:18–35. For instance, Paul is presented as a teacher in Acts 20:20, a significant aspect of the persona of Paul in the Pastorals (see 1 Tim 2:7 and 2 Tim 1:11; 4:7). His urgent exhortation in Acts 20:28 with its solemn pastoral charge finds echoes in 1 Timothy 6:20 and 2 Timothy 1:13–14 and 2:2. This is not evidence of common authorship but the existence of the activity of something like a Pauline school with access to the letters and to Acts.[2]

Klaus Wegenast (1962) surveys the understanding of tradition itself in the undisputed Paulines and the deutero-Pauline corpus, the Pastorals included (1962:132–57). In the former, Paul appeals to verbal traditions (such as 1 Cor 15:1–11) or cites literary traditions (such as Phil 2:5–11) he and his addressees know. These traditions originated independently of the apostle and are affirming witnesses of the unique and unmediated revelation that he received (see Gal 1:11–12). Paul takes a stance with respect to tradition that demonstrates that he is free with regard to it.

Turning to the Pastoral Epistles, Wegenast observes that the author is greatly concerned that his addressees guard the "deposit" (Gr.: *paratheke;* see 1 Tim 6:20; 2 Tim 1:14). Wegenast understands the "deposit" as the Pauline tradition: the whole Pauline heritage, now conceived as something immutable, laid down, to be protected and transmitted undiminished at all cost. This is the chief task of the officials of the churches. Whereas for

Paul the gospel he preached, which came by revelation, stood over all traditions (Gr.: *paradoseis*) as their norm, in the Pastorals the deposit stands over all contemporary articulations of the Pauline heritage. In the struggle with the early Gnostics, who were infecting the Pauline churches with their own interpretation of the Pauline heritage, the Pastorals are themselves actualizations of that deposit in written form. Moreover, the letters are powerful vehicles of an image of Paul who mandates the message embodied in the letters and sanctions the protecting and leadership role of ecclesiastical officials. Paul's heritage, to which the letters give voice, is to be passed on unchanged by the current leaders to faithful successors. Paul has become author and guarantor of the gospel (1 Tim 2:7; 2 Tim 2:8). As such, he authorizes the fight against the false teachers and is himself the chief weapon in the struggle to protect the Pauline identity of the churches.

The Role and Image of Paul

C. K. Barrett's brief book, *The Signs of an Apostle* (1970), devotes several perceptive pages to the Pastorals and their relationship to the apostle (1970:54–56). For Barrett, Paul is the persecuted "hero" of the letters. They allude to no other apostle. Nevertheless, the picture of Paul that emerges in the letters has more in common with the historical Paul than is generally supposed. 1 Timothy 2:7 and 2 Timothy 1:11 speak of Paul not only as apostle but also as "herald" (Gr.: *kerux*) and "teacher" (Gr.: *didaskalos*) "of the Gentiles" (1 Tim 2:7). While Paul did not use the two latter terms, he would have recognized the aptness of the ascription "herald." Barrett surmises that Paul deliberately did not use this term because of notions of sacrosanctity implicit in its use in the contemporary Greco-Roman environment (1970:54). By contrast, he fully recognized the necessity of suffering, perceiving that it was inescapably bound up with his apostolate. While employing the term "herald," the author of the Pastorals is fully cognizant of the suffering of Paul, most explicitly in 2 Timothy.

Other aspects of Paul's self-awareness are also encountered in the letters. Paul has an exalted view of his calling to be a preacher of the grace of God (1 Tim 1:11–16), even though he is the "chief of sinners." This is consonant with the historical Paul's painful awareness of his past (see, e.g., 1 Cor 15:9). The author is also aware of the need to safeguard the gospel (see Gal 1:8 and, e.g., 1 Tim 6:20), as well as the fact that the Christian life can be spoken about as "dying with Christ" (2 Tim 2:11; cf. Rom 6:3; Gal 2:19–20).

Martinus C. de Boer's incisive article, "Images of Paul in the Post-Apostolic Period" (1980), is one of several written by scholars in the 1970s and early 1980s on the theme of the image of Paul in the Pastorals (cf. Collins [1975]; Wilson [1976]; Hanson [1981]). The Pastoral Epistles represent a fuller development of the tendency in Ephesians and Colossians to regard Paul as the apostle par excellence (1980:364). Suffering, de Boer notes, is integral to the apostle's self-understanding in the undisputed letters (1 Cor 4:9–13; 2 Cor 4:7–12; Gal 6:14–17) and the Pastorals. In the latter, the apostle's suffering becomes the model for his successors; indeed, it is a definitive mark of true ministry (see 2 Tim 2:3; 3:12). Paul is also depicted in the Pastorals as a one-time persecutor of the church, a tradition which (in literary terms) originates in Acts and, in Paul's own words, Galatians 1:13, 23; Philippians 3:6; and 1 Corinthians 15:9. In common with Acts and Ephesians, the Pastorals use this well-known fact from the tradition in the struggle with false teachers to legitimate Paul as the exclusive apostle, teacher, and herald. His past serves to highlight his present exalted credentials. Paul, the prototypical sinner (1 Tim 1:15), received mercy from God to carry out the task of bringing the gospel to the world and to act as an example to all who believe. Far from encouraging an antinomian lifestyle, as de Boer believes the false teachers to be claiming, that gospel leads to godly living (1 Tim 1:16). Even if the Pastor has misunderstood the apostle's teaching on the law (or if it has ceased to be relevant), he knows that Paul's message is integrally bound up with it. This can be seen in the immediate affirmation of the purpose of the law at the beginning of

1 Timothy. When used rightly the law condemns blatantly evil behavior (see 1 Tim 1:8). The depiction of Paul as teacher (cf. Acts 20:20–21; 28:31) represents the fullest New Testament development of this concept.

The Pastoral Epistles as Actualizations of Pauline Tradition

There are hints in Barrett's and de Boer's studies of other aspects of the Pauline tradition that are expressed in the Pastorals. Peter Trummer develops these more fully in an important monograph published in 1978 (see also 1981:122–46). Trummer believes that one can only properly interpret the letters when one recognizes both their pseudepigraphical nature and their character as embodiments or actualizations of Pauline tradition. The Pastor actualizes literary and theological aspects of the Pauline tradition, adapting and transforming that tradition, and extending the authority of the apostle into a situation now discontinuous with that of the historical Paul. As such, the Pastorals are significant witnesses to the canonization of the Pauline corpus.

After examinations of recent scholarship on the authorship of the Pastoral Epistles, Trummer devotes Part III (1978:107–60) to a study of the literary affinities of the Pastorals with the Pauline corpus. He perceives many instances where the Pastor is unmistakably dependent on the wording encountered in the letters. The portrait of Timothy as an esteemed fellow worker, for example, owes much to his presentation in Philippians 2:19–22 and 1 Corinthians 4:17, as well as to 1 Corinthians 16:10 (cf. Titus in 2 Cor 8:23). The Pastor's injunction in 1 Timothy 2:11–12 regarding women teaching in the congregation is dependent on 1 Corinthians 14:33b–36. The "deception" of Eve mentioned by Paul in 2 Corinthians 11:3 is evoked in 1 Timothy 2:14. There are echoes of Acts as well. The difficulties encountered by Paul and his band recorded in, say, Acts 13:14, 51; 14:1, 6, 21 are seemingly alluded to in 2 Timothy. On two of the few occasions when the Pastor cites the Old Testament, there are comparisons to be made with Paul's use of the same passages.[3]

Part IV (1978:161–240) is devoted to an investigation of the shape Pauline theology takes in the Pastorals. The Pauline teaching on justification is admittedly not found in a recognizable form in the letters. However, the Pastor insists that believers are saved by God's grace and mercy and not "by works" (2 Tim 1:9; Titus 3:5). When Paul speaks of "works" he has "works of the law" in mind (see Gal 2:16; 3:1, 11, 24), namely, circumcision and the other marks of Jewish identity prescribed in the law. However, when the Pastor speaks of "works" he has taken the concept beyond the Jewish background so important for understanding Paul, and speaks either simply and generally of "works" (2 Tim 1:9) or of "works of righteousness" (Titus 3:5). In this he is to be compared with the author of Ephesians (see 2:8–9).[4] Pauline ideas are being loosed from their historical particularity. Trummer judges the Christology of the Pastorals as synthetic, containing both Pauline and non-Pauline elements. The suffering of Paul is clearly significant for the letters and is forcefully echoed, particularly in 2 Timothy. The ethics of the Pastorals owe much to the Pauline corpus. Trummer particularly stresses the fact that both Paul and the Pastor ground the conduct of the Christian life in the proclamation of Christ.[5] Consequently, the ethics of the letters is not to be understood as a compendium of conventional wisdom. While Paul's sense of the imminent parousia has receded somewhat, the Pastorals are closer to the undisputed letters in their awareness of future expectation than are the other deutero-Paulines.

Finally, in a concise summary of his argument (1978:241–50), Trummer protests that much scholarship on the letters has over-drawn the contrast between them and the rest of the Pauline corpus, with the result that the nature of the Pastorals as actualizations of Pauline tradition has been overshadowed. There is sufficient evidence to posit them as embodiments of a transformed Pauline tradition, furthering and legitimizing the reach of the apostle beyond his own historical particularity.

Gerhard Lohfink's essay "Paulinische Theologie in der Rezeption der Pastoralbriefe" (1981:70–121) affirms the thrust of Trummer's thesis. He also underscores a number of thematic links between the homologoumena and the Pastorals. Yet it is clear that the letters also develop these themes. While Paul does speak of himself as an example to his addressees (1 Cor 4:16; 11:1; Phil 3:17; 1 Thess 1:6; Gal 4:12), the Pastorals sharpen this aspect of Paul's paraenesis to caste him as the prototype of redeemed humankind (see 1 Tim 1:15). The letters do stress the suffering of the apostle and regard that suffering as integral to his apostleship, but little of Paul's self-confessed physical weakness (see, e.g., 2 Cor 12:8–10) is captured in them. Lohfink argues that the Gnostics, among whom are those polemicized in the letters, were not prepared to suffer.[6] In radical disagreement with Klaus Wegenast, Lohfink argues that the "deposit" to be guarded in the Pastorals is to be identified with the Pauline gospel, not the whole heritage of the apostle including his teaching and his injunctions as articulated in the letters (1981:101–2). What Wegenast understands as "deposit" the Pastor understands as "teaching" (Gr.: *didaskalia*).[7] This stress on the "teaching" is no invention of the author. Indeed, in the undisputed letters, Paul is much concerned about the "teaching" (see Rom 6:17; 16:17) and the "tradition" (1 Cor 15:3) he passes on to his congregations. Finally, Lohfink argues that the reference to the apostolic parousia in 1 Corinthians 4:16–17 provides the impetus for the author to underscore the role of Timothy and Titus as the substitutes for the living presence of the apostle. 1 Timothy 3:14–15 and 4:13 are quite explicit in this regard with respect to Timothy's role as he waits for Paul to arrive. The Pastor is thereby casting the addressees of the letters as very much the embodiments of Paul and guarantors of the Pauline character of the teaching they are charged to continue passing on to the congregations.

David G. Meade's approach to the Pastorals is part of a wider enterprise in which he integrates the production of pseudepigrapha with the transmission of tradition. In his book *Pseudonymity and*

Canon (1986) he advances the thesis that pseudepigrapha found in the Hebrew Bible, the literature of early Judaism, and the New Testament encapsulate a claim not of literary origins but of authoritative tradition. The Pastoral Epistles, he argues, articulate a strong sense of the need to guard and pass on the Pauline deposit. They contain an exclusive focus on Paul. He appears as the only apostle and—in contrast to the undisputed letters with their awareness of tradition that Paul receives from others—urges his addressees to adhere to what they have received from him (see 2 Tim 1:13). Consequently, the Christian identity of the addressees was, in Meade's words, "exclusively created and sustained by the figure of Paul" (1986:123). "For them," he continues, "Paul was not only a bearer of the proper tradition, but *part* of the tradition itself." For Meade, the question in the Pastorals is not so much the demonstration of Paul's authority, since both the addressees and false teachers accept it. Rather, the issue is the identity of the authoritative interpreters of Paul. Timothy and Titus, and the leadership associated with them in the past, present, and future, constitute an authoritative, legitimate, and unbroken line of interpreters stretching back to Paul himself. The pseudonymity of the letters, Meade concludes, extends the presence of Paul into the present and beyond. The letters mediate the "presence and word of Paul," and personalize the Pauline tradition (1986:137).

More than any other contemporary scholar, I suspect, Michael Wolter (1988) perceives just how significant is the Pastoral's presentation of Paul as the prototype of the saved person. Wolter contends that the Pauline communities for whom the letters were written were facing a crisis—teachers for whom Paul did *not* play a role were undermining their Pauline identity. These teachers espoused other theological traditions (1988:16). Consequently, the letters were written to secure the Pauline identity of these communities and to confirm their salvation. The Pastor presents Paul as the only legitimate interpreter and guarantor of salvation in Christ. The "call" of Paul to be an apostle has undoubted saving implications for all who come after him. Only insofar as Paul's praxis and teaching are followed and preserved can the communities be sure of gaining their salvation (1988:91, 95, 130). The letters, therefore, embody his presence and his claim to be the guarantor of their eschatological salvation. They clearly prescribe the need for faithful successors whose task it will be to preserve and keep the heritage inviolable and to teach it to faithful leaders who will succeed them. The content of the heritage is termed a "deposit" by the Pastor.[8] In contrast to Lohfink but in agreement with Wegenast, Wolter understands the "deposit" as wider in meaning than the Pauline gospel, the letters themselves encapsulating it.

Pauline Tradition Outside the New Testament

The role played by Pauline tradition in the second century, especially outside of the orthodox church, is being increasingly analyzed, thanks to the discovery and publication of the Nag Hammadi corpus, much of which has its origin in the Gnostic teacher Valentinus and his followers. Until recently scholars did not have access to Gnostic writings except through citations preserved in their opponents, chiefly Irenaeus, Tertullian, and Epiphanius. For Valentinus, Paul was "the" apostle (Pagels 1975:2; Bauer 1971:224–25; Barrett 1973–74:236–37; de Boer 1980:363). Not only does Valentinus know and use Pauline letters, he lays claim to the apostle's esoteric teaching. This teaching, it was claimed, had been transmitted to his pupil, Theudas and thence to Valentinus (Clem. *Strom.* 7.17; ANF 2.555). In her book, *The Gnostic Paul* (1975), Elaine Pagels demonstrates how influential Pauline letters were to the Gnostics. The extreme rarity of the Valentinians' use of the Pastorals contrasts with the frequency of their citations of other letters of the corpus (Hebrews included).[9] Indeed, the list of letters that seems to be regarded as authoritative is co-extensive with the collection extant in P46—the Pastorals, Philemon, and 2 Thessalonians are not cited (1975:5). Pagels contends that the three Pastorals were written ca. 100–110 to counteract heretical tendencies and to enlist Paul as an organizer of ecclesiastical communities (1975:163).

In his *Orthodoxy and Heresy in Earliest Christianity* (1971) Walter Bauer observes that earliest Christianity existed in a plurality of forms.[10] What later "orthodox" fathers condemned as "heresy" had not been such at all originally, but had existed in certain locations (particularly in the east) from the beginning as the only form of the new faith (1971:xxii). He advances the bold thesis that by the end of the second century the Roman church, galvanized by its victory over the interloper Marcion (who had arrived in Rome in 138 C.E.), had been instrumental in the formation of the "great" church. As a result, Christianity was neatly divided into one orthodox church founded by the apostles—preserving the original deposit of the Christian faith that it had received from Christ himself—and diverse heretical groupings. The Pastorals, he argues, were written to counter the use of Paul and his letters by false teachers and to rehabilitate him for the "orthodox," few of whom were prepared to cite him before Irenaeus. The letters are testimony to a titanic struggle for the identity of the church and for the reclamation of Paul in the face of his use by Marcion (1971:226).

Few scholars have followed Bauer's reconstruction of the second-century influence of Rome in the rise of orthodoxy or his dating of the Pastorals. However, many scholars today contend that there were custodians of Pauline tradition outside the orthodox church. They believe that these custodians of Paul were silenced. Paul's authority was marshaled against them. The Pastorals embody a particularly effective counter to their positions. The extant written deposit of postapostolic, but extracanonical, writings, much of it claiming a Pauline pedigree, has come under increased scrutiny in the interests of elucidating marginalized trajectories of early Christianity. This investigation has coincided with the debate over the role of women in the modern church. The knowledge that there were early Christian communities—chiefly Marcionite, Gnostic, and Montanist—in which celibate women ministered with equal authority and status with men has placed the Pastorals, which forth-rightly deny such a role to women, in the forefront of much recent scholarly endeavor.[11] Consequently, the late-second-century *Acts of Paul* has attracted considerable attention as a possible actualization of the Pauline tradition which sanctions women's access to positions of leadership in the church.

Virgins and Widows

Since the 1970s a vast literature has been accumulating on this topic. Rosemary Radford Ruether's article "Misogynism and Virginal Feminism in the Fathers of the Church" (1974:150–83) is an excellent place to begin. She demonstrates from the later fathers, chiefly Jerome and Augustine, how virginity and sexual continence came to be highly esteemed in the orthodox church. The fathers argued that the virginal and continent states, which require that self-control for which women were regarded as noto-riously ill-equipped, are anticipations of the resurrection life. Such a lifestyle might be preferred over married life with its sub-jection to a husband and the pain and danger of childbirth. But on no account should such women presume to act independently of male sanction, a point that Tertullian, for example, hammers home in his *On Baptism* and elsewhere.[12] However, sections of the early church of the second and third centuries do testify to continent women acting independently and in considerable ten-sion with social conventions.

Stevan L. Davies' monograph *The Revolt of the Widows* (1980) explores the role of "widows," a technical term that includes unmarried virgins (1980:72; cf. Ign. *Smyrn.* 13:1), in the apoc-ryphal *Acts*. These date from ca. 160–225 C.E. The *Acts of Paul* is the best known of these, a work that Elisabeth Schüssler Fiorenza claims was widely regarded as canonical in sections of the early church (1979:51; 1983:53, 173). Davies observes that the *Acts* all assume that sexual continence is a constituent aspect of the Chris-tian life. "Widows" comprise a distinct grouping in many early church communities, including the churches of the Pastorals. They are the subject of a substantial regulatory injunction in 1 Timothy 5:3–16. Davies surmises that the *Acts* were written by literate members of these communities to keep alive this celibate and semi-clerical lifestyle as an authentic expression of the apostolic faith (1980:30, 108).[13] The apostles who appear in these works are presented as opponents of the conventional social order and the means of social control, the "widows" escaping from patriarchal power and conventional household structures (1980:32).[14] That the tradition represented in the *Acts* was perceived as subversive can be seen in the response of many of the early fathers.

Jouette M. Bassler's article "The Widow's Tale: A Fresh Look at 1 Tim. 5:3–16" (1983:23–41) draws similar conclusions. Christianity began as an egalitarian movement (see also Thurston 1989:39). The apostle Paul sanctioned equality of men and women (see Gal 3:28) and preferred celibacy to the married state (see 1 Cor 7:8–9, 25–28) (1983:24; cf. Barclay 1997:72–78). The tradition of Paul's asceticism, one followed by the "widows," amounted to a liberating choice of lifestyle. Although Paul does issue injunctions that express his desire for church order, the post-Pauline household codes *(Haustafeln),* while retaining something of Paul's notion of gender equality, place greater emphasis on the obedience and submission of subordinate members of the household, summoning them to reflect social convention (1983:30). The Pastoral Epistles are part of the early post-Pauline attempt to re-inculcate social expectations in congregations that kept alive something of the fraternal spirit to be seen operating in the churches Paul founded. Consequently, in 1 Timothy 5:3–16, "widows" are brought closely under the purview of the institutionalized leadership of the churches. While the Pastor affirms their lifestyle, he exhorts younger "widows" to marry. Evidence of the conventional domestic virtues becomes a significant criterion for enrollment. Any presumption on the part of these women to preach and teach in the congregation is totally curtailed. Bassler aptly concludes her study with the observation that in the

Pastorals a "potentially objectionable force [i.e., the "widows"] has been tamed" (1983:38; Thurston 1989:107).

In *A New Song: Celibate Women in the First Three Centuries* (1983) Jo Ann McNamara contrasts the subversive teaching of Jesus on family obligations with later Christian writers' attempts to strengthen the traditional patriarchal family order and to enforce roles of women as daughters, wives, and mothers. The gospel record, she writes, preserves Jesus' attacks on the institutional, patriarchal family and embodies what she calls "a clear incitement to rebellion against the power of the family" (1983:51). Moreover, Jesus delineates a set of values that re-envision the typical feminine experience of powerlessness, humility, and poverty as positive virtues (1983:27). John Barclay (1997:66–80, esp. 72–78) similarly observes that, in the early Christian movement, the ascetic ideal in which family life is fundamentally renounced and commitment to traditional family structures exist together as contrasting trajectories. 1 Corinthians 7 testifies to the existence of these two traditions in Corinth. It is striking to note just how much Paul agreed with the ascetic option (1997:75). However, the Pastorals seek to circumscribe the lifestyle of the members of the church through the structures and conventions of the household alone. Yet, 1 Timothy 4:3 shows that the rejection of marriage and family life continued to be seen as an influential option in some early Christian circles.

Margaret MacDonald (1996) has considered second-century non-Christian observations as well as biblical and early Christian texts relevant to the role of women in the church. From her study of writers such as Pliny, Galen, and Celsus, she concludes that there is good evidence of women taking leadership roles. She also confirms the conclusions of other scholars that Paul's response to the role of celibate women in the Corinthian church is indeed relaxed but he expresses respect for conventional household structures. Unlike the Pastor, however, Paul does not limit the choices to remain unmarried to older widows of a certain economic status who have raised children (1996:152; cf. 1 Tim 5:9, 10). However, the Pastorals bear witness to a time when criticism of the potential for celibate women to bring shame on the community results in the prescription that the private world of the believers "visibly conform to public standards" (1996:178). *The Acts of Paul* is a testimony to the continued attraction of the tradition that associated celibacy and renunciation of marriage with the ministry of Paul (1996:170).

Dennis R. MacDonald's monograph *The Legend and the Apostle: The Battle for Paul in Story and Canon* (1983) proposes a substantial relationship between the *Acts of Paul* and the Pastoral Epistles.[15] He argues that the Pastor wrote the letters to counter the image of Paul presented by women who disseminated oral traditions and legends about Paul, such as those found in the *Acts*. These storytellers remembered Paul as one who ordained women to preach and teach, and who sanctioned a liberating and continent lifestyle in the face of the social expectations women were expected to fulfill. The Pastor not only knew these traditions, he specifically wrote to oppose them, seeking to silence these women and their stories (1983:14). In contrast to their portrait of Paul as one who sanctioned what amounted to social deviance (and an anti-Roman stance), the Pastor presented Paul as a social conservative, a political quiescent, and a submissive martyr. Whereas the women followed an ascetic, celibate lifestyle and presumed to teach in the congregation, even to prophesy, the Pastorals vilify them as liars who are attending to deceitful spirits and teachings of demons (1 Tim 4:1). Against asceticism, the Pastor insists that creation is inherently good (1 Tim 4:4). Marriage is not to be forbidden. Indeed, childbearing is the means of salvation for women (1 Tim 2:15). Women are forbidden to teach in the congregation (1 Tim 2:12). Presbyter/bishops are to be married, male householders (1 Tim 3:2, 4; Titus 1:6). Moreover, as other scholars observe, the Pastor limits the role of the "widows" in the church, curtailing enrollment in the order (1 Tim 5:9) and restricting their teaching to younger women. The curriculum is narrowed to the inculcation of domestic virtues and the need to render submission to one's husband (1983:73–77; cf. Titus 2:3b–5).

MacDonald's thesis has not persuaded all. However, many scholars would agree that the *Acts* and the Pastorals represent contrasting ways in which early Christian communities remembered Paul. We can no longer assume, MacDonald observes, that the letters (together with the other New Testament deutero-Pauline letters and the Acts of the Apostles) were the only bearers of the legacy of Paul in the post-Pauline era. In fact, MacDonald makes a case for the preservation in the Acts of something of the memory of Paul as an apocalypticist (1983:98). The prophetesses of the second century and the story-telling women remembered Paul as "a fanatical, marginal social type" (1983:89). In contrast to the socially conservative image preserved in the Pastorals, Paul, as remembered by the women, preached and modeled sexual equality, encouraged the manumission of slaves, and included women as partners with him in his missionary enterprise. However, the Pastorals do perceive the dangers of sectarianism and mandate social and theological stances that allow for a greater sense of continuity between the wider society and the church.

Responses

There are scholarly voices raised in protest against the theory that the *Acts of Paul* is a repository of genuine Pauline tradition reaching back to the life of the apostle himself. Margaret Howe (1980) argues that in the *Acts,* Paul, far from bestowing on Thecla a substantial teaching ministry, grants her a limited role, largely directed toward women and predicated upon considerable self-abnegation on Thecla's part (1980:42). She feels constrained to dress like a man, cut her hair, and forsake marriage. The historical Paul, on the other hand, assumed that women were equal partners in his mission, even if he did prescribe certain dress requirements for the exercise of the gift of prophecy. He did not require celibacy, though he personally preferred the state. For Paul, celibacy was a reasonable choice of lifestyle not because it granted freedom from male domination and/or oppressive social convention, but because of the eschatological urgency of the times.[16] The *Acts,* therefore, is more restrictive in its view of the ministry and leadership of women, preserves a "pale reflection" of the kind of woman leader we encounter in the Pauline letters, and marks a retreat from the historical Paul's affirmations of women (1980:46–47).

Lynne C. Boughton's provocative article on the *Acts of Paul* (1991:362–83; cf. Dunn 1993:245–61) is particularly critical of Elisabeth Schüssler Fiorenza, Dennis MacDonald, and other scholars, who, she claims, read modern feminist concerns into the texts we are considering and detect extracanonical Pauline tradition more faithfully preserved in the *Acts* than in the post-Pauline letters. Boughton argues that the *Acts* is a hagiography written to underscore the sanctity of Thecla, who attracted a popular cult following in the early church. Boughton argues that second-century cultural concerns imbue the *Acts.* Its author knows nothing substantial of the first-century Christian context, except a passing acquaintance with some historical figures, events, and controversies from the New Testament era (1991:363). The author is not occupied with transmitting Pauline traditions as though supplementing or redefining the canonical deposit. Contrary to Schüssler Fiorenza, Boughton argues that the *Acts* was not regarded as canonical in some sections of the early church since nowhere is there any testimony that the *Acts* was regarded as normative for establishing apostolic teaching (1991:367). To the assertion that the book preserves suppressed apostolic sanction for the leadership of women in the church, Boughton, in company with Howe, responds that the role of Thecla is limited. She baptizes herself in the arena in expectation of her martyrdom. Her alleged teaching ministry is nothing more than that of an itinerant instructing potential converts, mostly women. She does not exercise any leadership or spiritual direction in a congregation. She is not carrying out a baptizing ministry. There is nothing to suggest in the *Acts* that Thecla's ministry is anything other than what was approved by the fathers—who certainly approved celibacy and affirmed the (albeit limited) role of "widows" in a congregation—or, indeed, in the Pastorals (1991:376–77; cf. Titus 2:3b–5). Nevertheless, both Boughton and Howe overlook the fact that Tertullian was outraged that some women were appealing to the *Acts of Paul* as justification for presuming to teach and to baptize.

Conclusion

Scholars generating studies of the literary and theological relationship between the Pauline corpus and the Pastoral Epistles have built on the research of those who have sought to demonstrate their pseudonymity. Scholars such as Trummer and Lohfink have shown that the Pastorals can well claim to be actualizing Pauline tradition found in the Pauline corpus and, to a lesser extent, in the Acts of the Apostles. They seek not to distance the Pastor from Paul but to trace the development of the tradition beyond the career of the historical Paul into an era in which his churches faced problems and contingencies that were discontinuous with those Paul addressed. These scholars seek to show that the Pauline heritage was crafted to speak afresh—the apostle's authority and thought invoked for a "new day." The subsequent history of the canon shows that Paul and his literary deposit were in fact reclaimed in the face of their use by teachers, who were, I believe, custodians of a different interpretation of the Pauline heritage. The Pastor is polemically engaged with these teachers as he sought to secure the Pauline identity of his addressees.

Recent debate concerning the relationship between the late-second-century *Acts of Paul* and the Pastorals has been much exercised by the question of whether or not the *Acts* preserves traditions of the kind polemicized by the Pastor in ca. 100 C.E. This debate, as we have seen, is part of a general investigation of hierarchical, familial, and social values in the early Christian era and the alleged subversion of these values on the part of literate Christian women who chose a celibate lifestyle.

The question of whether Pauline tradition is actually found in the *Acts of Paul,* as well as in the Gnostic deposit, has raised important issues relating to the contours of the social setting of the Pastorals. We now turn to that setting.

3
The Social Setting
of the Pastoral Epistles

Introduction

The first two chapters of this book have largely concentrated on the Pastorals as articulations of ideas and theological concepts. Only briefly have we encountered social realities behind the documents. There remains a role for the analysis of the Pastorals in relation to Pauline tradition insofar as questions of their authorship can be profitably arbitrated in relation to the theology of the other Pauline letters.

Leander E. Keck's article "On the Ethos of the Early Christians" (1974:435–52) is a reminder that the faith of early believers was subject to social factors, and that theological discourse reflects social experience. By "ethos," Keck denotes the lifestyle of early Christians. A concern for their ethos requires us to orient ourselves to communities and social institutions, "seeing individuals in relation to them" (1974:440). The highly contextualized theological and ethical discourse encountered in Paul's letters is the result of a dialectic shaped by the ethos of the communities he addressed, an ethos that was itself shaped by socially determined factors. In the passage of time, the continually transforming ethos of the post-Pauline communities invited new actualizations of the Pauline heritage. Theology should no longer be written independently of ethics and sociology since, Keck argues, "the theologies of the New Testament were wrought in the matrix of an ethos undergoing diverse crises" (1974:451).

This chapter reviews the work of scholars who have sought to investigate the ethos of the addressees of the Pastorals as those inhabiting wider communities and participating in social institutions.

Social Institutions

What can we know of the social setting of the Pauline mission? The most convenient place to begin is Edwin A. Judge's *The Social Pattern of the Christian Groups in the First Century* (1960a). In a remarkably fertile analysis, Judge, a historian of Rome, notes that the New Testament churches took root in cities whose political autonomy was now, to use Judge's terms, "compromised" by Roman "supervision." In the New Testament era, power came to be increasingly concentrated in the hands of the well-to-do few, the more easily to guarantee the quality of Roman rule. There was a concomitant sense that the older, more democratic and accessible political institutions of the cities were increasingly unable to foster and enhance the social cohesion of the wider populace. Judge suggests that membership of the household and participation in its more intimate social benefits and ordered harmonies served as compensation (1960a:29).

The household was the basic social unit of Greco-Roman society. It comprised the extended family of the head together with servants and tenants. Former slaves (freedmen) of the household head became clients, with the head as their patron. The household was hierarchically ordered. Its order was sanctioned by and enshrined in venerable social convention and law. The head of the household was obliged to protect and to provide for his dependents, who, in turn, were obliged to fulfill their duties within the household structure and its economy. The household model even served as the basis of the relationship between the emperor as patron and his imperial subjects as clients. The house-hold, as the New Testament abundantly testifies, was the natural social context in which the new faith was propagated and in which believers met. Judge notes that New Testament writers (and here the Pastor is an important contributor) adapt household terminology to express theological concepts and to articulate ideas about the relationship between believers to one another and to God. Thus, believers are God's servants. Their leaders are his stewards whose duty it is to administer his goods for the benefit of his household. Nevertheless, Judge observes, republican politi-cal institutions and the household both served a "paternalistic order" (1960a:38). Democratic impulses, now almost totally eclipsed in the cities, were more likely to be realized in voluntary associations in which members participated as equals.

The associations were religious in tenor. They were organ-ized, for example, for charitable ends or to provide security of burial. Officials were elected. The associations were beyond the supervision of the political authorities, unless they attracted atten-tion through immorality or lapses of public order. Judge suggests that early Christian communities had sufficiently much in com-mon with the religious associations to have been perceived as such by outsiders.[1]

Judge's analysis of the social class of New Testament believers sees evidence of the propagation of the original Palestinian Messianic faith by what he describes as "a very cul-tivated section of international Jewry" (1960a:57). These Jews not only translated that faith effectively for the population of the hellenistic cities but also enjoyed the hospitality and sup-port of wealthy patrons over the whole compass of the eastern Mediterranean. The career of Paul bears remarkable testimony to this phenomenon. Patrons along the way—both men and women of means—greatly aided his traveling and that of his colleagues. These patrons, Judge argues, might be aptly said to have "sponsored" the Christian faith to their dependents (1960a:60, 76).[2]

Taking the church at Corinth as a typical example, Judge argues from New Testament evidence that the ranks of Christians "were dominated by a socially pretentious section of the population of the big cities" (1960a:60). The members of the churches were representative of a broad cross section of the city population. However, the owner and patron class had an interest in the maintenance of order in the communities. Paul finds himself inculcating limits to the license that many might have been tempted to claim, as 1 Corinthians 7:20–24 demonstrates. Membership of an association of equals did not sanction the subversion of the conventional hierarchy of the household. Fraternity and hierarchy exist in tension in the Pauline letters (cf. Barclay 1997:72–78).

The early Christian communities are well aware of the need to maintain good order. Judge speaks of the existence of an "acute sensitivity to public opinion" in the New Testament, sensitivity that springs from insecurity as much from the eschatological faith the believers espouse. Consequently, Judge determines that New Testament social thought is "formulated primarily for defense rather than attack," lest any abnormal or socially deviant behavior attract the attention of outsiders (1960a:73). The Pastorals evidence considerable anxiety about public opinion. The "ecclesiastical machinery" is tightened up in order to more effectively prevent moral lapses and outbreaks of social deviance. While the household offered believers "the best possible security" for their existence as a group, there was always the risk that that cohesion could be fractured by enthusiasm. There was potential for bringing down the wrath of the authorities if there were "political indiscretions or offences against the hierarchy of the household" (1960a:76).

Scholars since have taken up the challenge outlined by Judge to define the social institutions of the hellenistic cities of New Testament times.[3] A number have published monographs that are particularly relevant for the study of the social setting of the Pastorals.

"The Household of God"

It has long been recognized that certain passages in the New Testament letters—Ephesians 5:22—6:9; Colossians 3:18—4:1; 1 Peter 2:13—3:8; 1 Timothy 2:8–15; 5:1–2; 6:1–2; and Titus 2:1–10; 3:1–2—reflect an interest in the responsibilities and duties of members of the household. These are part of a common tradition in Greco-Roman and earlier philosophical discourse originating with Plato and Aristotle. The duties of the members are presented in a codified and standardized form constituting a well-defined "topic" *(topos)* in the wider philosophical analysis of the obligation of individuals to the political structures of the city-state.

In 1981, David L. Balch published a monograph devoted to the Greco-Roman background of the household code *(Haustafel)* of 1 Peter 2:18—3:9 and its function in that letter. He built on several earlier explorations of the household theme in New Testament scholarship (chiefly Crouch [1972] and Thraede [1977]). Though focused on 1 Peter, the benefit of Balch's work for understanding the Pastorals is to locate the tradition of the *Haustafeln* in earlier philosophical discourse on household management. This discourse considered the management, authority structure, and ordering of the household as well as the appropriate duties of each member within the wider context of the political order of the state.[4] In the deutero-Pauline and later New Testament letters in which the *topos* is articulated, Christian writers self-consciously adapt the traditional content in paraenetic address to their communities. In each case, the New Testament authors are concerned lest the traditional hierarchical ordering of the household, and hence the state, be subverted by any failure on the part of the subordinate members to fully uphold the conventions and expectations of their station.

Balch, in common with Judge, notes longstanding Roman sensitivity to the potential for the subversion of the household posed by the participation of women and slaves in oriental cults and gives numerous examples of the offense and outrage caused by their involvement. He argues that the Roman ruling classes, as guardians of the social order, would have been particularly sensitive to any charge brought against Christians with respect to undermining household conventions. The presence of the codes in the New Testament, Balch argues, is evidence not of the diminishing eschatological expectation in the churches, as has often been argued,[5] but of the response to actual or potential criticism on the part of outsiders who expected that all members of society accept Roman social-political customs (1981:106).

More recently, Balch and Carolyn Osiek have produced a lucid account of the Greco-Roman household entitled *Families in the New Testament World: Households and House Churches* (1997). The book deals first with relevant archaeological sites and literary sources for the social environment of the Greco-Roman household and proceeds to a discussion of early Christian families and house churches. The authors uphold the results of earlier New Testament research that have underscored the patriarchal structure of the ideal household and the perceived inferiority of women, children, and slaves in the household economy. Given the widespread belief that women were notoriously unable to control their sexual passions, thereby potentially plunging the entire household into shame and dishonor, it was necessary that women be "controlled, enclosed, and guarded" as far as possible (1997:40). Balch and Osiek argue that the presence of the household management *topos* in the deutero-Pauline letters, the Pastorals included, represents acculturation on the part of the writers to the prevailing patriarchal social conventions of the cities and towns of the empire. The codes herald the eclipse of the emancipist and fraternal tendencies existing in somewhat uneasy tension in the earlier Pauline churches in which some women did host house churches. We know of Chloe (1 Cor 1:11), Prisca (with Aquila, 1 Cor 16:19; Rom 16:5) and Nympha (Col 4:15) who shouldered this responsibility. Other women participated on an equal footing with Paul in his mission (see Rom 16:3, 6, 12; Phil 4:2–3).[6] Others prayed and prophesied (1 Cor 11:5, 13) or fulfilled offices, even that of apostle

(Junia [or Julia], Rom 16:7). In Romans 16:1, Phoebe is termed a patron (Gr.: *prostatis*) as well as a "deacon," an office consonant with that of the two female slaves (termed *ministrae*) whom Pliny tortured in his interrogation of Christians in Bithynia ca. 110 (*Epistles* x.96 [8]).

David C. Verner has largely affirmed Balch's earlier conclusions regarding the provenance and function of the household code in his 1983 monograph *The Household of God: The Social World of the Pastoral Epistles.* Basing his investigation on the statement in 1 Timothy 3:14–15, Verner argues that the author of the Pastorals sets forth a "coherent concept of the church as the household of God." The author of the letters contends that the household is the basic social unit of the church and that the church itself is "a social structure modeled on the household" (1983:1). Polemic in the letters (see 2 Tim 3:6; Titus 1:10–11) is directed toward those who would undermine good order by provoking social tensions within the church household. In agreement with Balch, Verner argues that the church is being accused of subverting the political structures of the state and underscores Judge's and Balch's assessments of the sensibilities of the Roman ruling class toward unrest in the household. He believes that the same anxieties were held in common throughout the empire because the traditional patriarchal structure of the household would have been considered integral in maintaining the good order of the whole society and, ultimately, the *pax Romana* itself (1983:76).

Verner notes that New Testament writers use of the household management *topos* to exhort the superior and inferior members of the churches. Despite the fact that the codes all use traditional material, there is also evidence of the specific situations being addressed. He also notes that the Pastorals, like Polycarp, *Letter to the Philippians* 4.2—6.1 (cf. Ign. *Pol.* 4), have transformed and extended the code addressed to members of the household family (as in 1 Pet 2—3; Eph 5; and Col 3) to include the different categories of members of the church, resulting in what he and von Campenhausen (1963:230) term a "station" code. 1 Timothy 2:1—6:1 and, more concisely, Titus 2:1–10 are, in effect, "station" codes (Verner 1983:83–111).

Verner observes that the leadership cadre of the churches is clearly restricted to the ranks of senior, well-to-do, though well-qualified, (male) householders. Their rule over the church house-hold is analogous to their rule over their family households. Married women are exhorted to cultivate the virtues of domesticity and modesty, and to aspire to the sober station of the Roman matron. Any teaching by women in the congregation is forbidden, the Pastor mounting a devastatingly powerful argument against their presumption.[7] Here Verner perceives a contrast between the emancipist *Acts of Paul* and the Pastorals, observing that the author of the latter condemns the rejection of marriage and forbids women a congregational teaching ministry. On the other hand, the *Acts* upholds the rejection of marriage and promotes a teaching ministry for women (1983:178). Support for "real" widows, their upkeep being arduous for the church (see 1 Tim 5:16b), is relegated to "faithful women" (v16a), the very women from whose ranks the many entrepreneurial sponsors of the earlier mission of Paul would have come. Slaves are exhorted to obey their masters, lest the "name of God and the teaching be blasphemed" (1 Tim 6:1).

In the Pastorals, leadership ministries have ceased to be charismatically endowed. The Spirit is now bestowed at the laying on of hands of qualified householders. Verner surmises that women and ambitious younger males, not to mention slaves, are now to be excluded from the cadre. It was they, Verner suggests, as the subordinate groups in the church household, who are the adherents and promoters of the false teaching polemicized against in the Pastorals. In response, the letters stress the necessity of subscribing to the social values of urban Greco-Roman society. The leadership of the church, God's household, Verner writes, "shared the same aristocratic social aspirations in the smaller sphere" (1983:160). Yet the churches of the Pastorals remain an arena for the exhibiting of social tensions that had existed from the beginning of the Pauline mission.[8] These, as Judge and Balch have also

argued, posed potentially disastrous consequences for the continued presence of the church in an anxious world always alert to
social deviance. The Pastor met the challenge by "promoting an
image of the church that legitimates the hierarchical structure"
(1983:186).[9] His sympathies are emphatically with the leadership
and the ranks of the householders.

"Bourgeois Christianity"

Balch, Osiek, and Verner have highlighted the central role
of the Greco-Roman household in the Pastorals. They have illuminated the ethical vision of the letters. That vision is integrally
related to the social values enshrined in the Greco-Roman household as the proper model for the church. The author crafts a
largely defensive strategy, one employed in the face of potential
and even actual accusations of social deviance leveled by munici-
pal and Roman authorities against the church. However, that
strategy has a positive aspect insofar as it does allow the church to
continue its witness more effectively.

The perception that the letters adopt and affirm such values
has long been held. In the first half of the twentieth century, Martin Dibelius developed the influential theory that the Pastorals
articulate what he (anachronistically) termed "bourgeois Christianity" *(bürgerliches Christentum).* The letters seek to inculcate
the values of good citizenship among believers in the light of the
waning of eschatological expectation. In contrast with the Pauline
homologoumena, the parousia is no longer perceived as imminent. The author of the Pastorals, Dibelius argues, is seeking to
"build the possibility of life in this world," envisioning such life
based on Christian principles (Dibelius-Conzelmann 1972:39).
As in Luke-Acts, Dibelius contends, the "ethics of good citizenship serve to regulate the time until the parousia" (Dibelius-
Conzelmann 1972:40). The asceticism of the Gnostics is
decisively rejected. The letters are in the process of developing a

family ethic that goes beyond the traditional injunctions of rules for the household.

Dibelius believes that the addressees of the letters were socially emergent with "bourgeois" aspirations. He assumes that their predecessors in the Pauline churches originated from the urban underclass. This has been decisively repudiated by the research of Judge and others since 1960 who argue that those who might be termed socially pretentious dominated early urban Christian communities from the beginning (Judge 1960a:49–61; Theissen 1982:69–119; Meeks 1983:51–77).

The first monograph to subject Dibelius's thesis to extensive analysis is Roland Schwarz's *Bürgerliches Christentum im Neuen Testament?* (1983). Schwarz believes that the Pastorals, for all their insistence on not giving offense to outsiders, are not as "bourgeois" as one might first suspect. He argues that the letters are intentionally allied with Greco-Roman exhortation as a strategy to counter the influence of false teachers, whose unorthodoxy, it is suggested, is expressed in their lack of commitment to conventional social standards. The letters inculcate the accepted ethical virtues not because the letters are accommodationist, but because only in this way will the church manage to differentiate itself from the values of the false teachers. The ministers of the Pastorals, rather than being founders and maintainers of a church seeking to become an institution, are protectors of the Pauline identity of the churches addressed in the letters. The bestowal of the Spirit on those set apart for congregational leadership and the eclipse of the indiscriminately endowed charismatic ministries of the Pauline churches do not mean the onset of an institutionalized "early Catholicism." Rather, this is a legitimate outworking of regulatory tendencies that can be traced to Paul himself, especially in 1 Corinthians (1983:156, 158). The regulations of the Pastorals for church life and order are not to be interpreted as indications of waning expectation of an imminent parousia, but are the result of the struggle against false teachers. Indeed, the ethical exhortations

are grounded in eschatological motivation. Schwarz understands the teaching of the Pastorals with respect to social convention as legitimate extensions of Paul's own teaching. In this,
the Pastor poses a radically different vision of church life than
that represented by the charismatically oriented false teachers.
They propounded a countervision of Christian society, which
took the baptismal formula of Galatians 3:28 as its charter, in
which all are equal (1983:162; cf. Betz 1979:184). Being a
Christian, Schwarz counters, has to do with living in the world
and in accord with its structures, presumably even those that
are hierarchical, in the duties of everyday life (cf. Karris
1979:xvii).

While Schwarz offers modifications of the "bourgeois
Christianity" theory of Dibelius, Philip Towner is much more
critical. In his monograph *The Goal of Our Instruction* (1989)
he contends that neither Dibelius and his followers nor even
Roland Schwarz have understood the true intent of the ethical
teaching of the Pastorals. The theory implies that the letters are
little more than accommodationist, that they are documents
urging peaceful co-existence with the world, and that they
amount to a "compromise" and "merger" with the values of the
world (1989:15) Towner argues that the goal of the ethics of the
Pastorals—a goal that Dibelius classifies as "bourgeois"—is in
fact intended to further the evangelistic mission of the church.
At stake in the mind of the author of the letters is not just the
church's existence, but also its mission. Although he interacts
minimally with scholars of the social context of the letters,
Towner does acknowledge the author's adaptation of the
household management *topos* in 1 Timothy and Titus. In company with many scholars, he interprets the author's use of
themes of the *topos* as expressing his commitment to the values
of urban Greco-Roman society of the Pastorals' addressees.
However, this is a proactive, not merely apologetic, strategy
designed to enhance evangelistic enterprise.[10]

The Pastoral Epistles and the Wealthy

Two stimulating monographs have appeared that take up the role of the wealthy in the Pastorals and the letters' attitude toward wealth. The first of these, L. William Countryman's *The Rich Christian in the Church of the Early Empire* (1980), surveys Christian attitudes toward wealth, setting that research in the social context of the authors and their churches. He confirms the observation noted above that membership of the early church was not drawn from one single social order or economic status. As far as one can gather from early Christian literature, the church "included rich and poor, privileged and non-privileged" (1980:33). The presence of the rich in the church gave rise to tensions and problems.

Countryman notes that the wealthy were expected to give alms, supporting the poor and needy in the congregations. The church, he maintains, needed the wealthy and could not afford to alienate them, though the rich were often portrayed as marginal Christians and potential apostates. "Alms," he writes, "were the cement of unity that bound people together within the individual congregation and bound congregations together within the ecumenical church" (1980:118). In certain respects, the church needed the wealth of the rich in a manner analogous to the city-state. Benefactions bestowed upon the citizenry were the usual means of distributing wealth in Greco-Roman society. However, benefactors expected a return in the form of honors measured in part by inscriptions and the conferral of status and privilege. Benefactors were motivated by "love of public recognition" (Gr.: *filotimia*). The benefaction system was thus a reciprocal civic phenomenon. It benefited citizens and the state, and, in turn, the benefactors themselves.[11]

Countryman maintains that the rich also endangered the church, partly because of the contempt they might show their social inferiors and partly because of the potential for insubordination toward legitimate church authorities. The Pastorals, Countryman argues, present just this scenario. The authority of Paul's delegates, Timothy and Titus, emanates from an outside source. There is evidence that wealthy women presumed to teach in the congregation (see 1 Tim 2:9–10) in breach of the order the author seeks to institute. At the end of 1 Timothy, the author tells the rich what their role in the church should be. They are to support the church generously by giving alms. They are not to "compete with the properly constituted authorities" (1980:154).

However, the rich Christian, Countryman argues, would have expected his role in the church to be similar to the one his non-Christian peers played in the religious associations or clubs. As patrons they were expected to meet the financial needs of the club. In return, inscriptions recorded honors bestowed in return by the grateful members. Club officers had little freedom to alter the terms of donations. However, in the church, the donations of the rich were fully controlled by the clergy. Whereas in the club honors were regularly bestowed upon generous patrons, no honors were paid "patrons" in the churches. The clergy, moreover, might be appointed for life, as in *1 Clement* 44.2–3. In the club, the wealthy could expect to be elected to various positions. Thus, the potential for tension was considerable. In effect, the author of the Pastorals co-opts wealthy (male) householders into the ranks of the clergy, as long as they fit the criteria. "All ranks of ministers," Countryman observes, "are expected to display the virtues appropriate to prosperous householders" (1980:181 n.42). It is not unexpected that in the second and third centuries many bishops show evidence of considerable wealth.

Reggie M. Kidd's *Wealth and Beneficence in the Pastoral Epistles* (1990) is largely concerned with Dibelius's "bourgeois Christianity" theory. At a number of points he registers his indebtedness to Countryman (1980) and Verner (1983), as well as Judge (1960a). Kidd tackles Dibelius's view that the Pastorals enshrine an ethic that is "culturally accommodative" and "unheroically conservative," and that the culturally critical stance of Paul has been replaced by an accommodationist stance.

Kidd neatly dispatches the contention that the addressees of the Pastorals are socially ascendant, in that sense "bourgeois." He argues that the Pauline mission had had success among such people from its beginning. Taking his cue from Countryman, he suggests that wealthy believers might have seen themselves as belonging to a kind of religious association or club, expecting to fulfill roles in the church analogous to the ones they and their peers filled in the club. However, the Pastorals make it clear that wealth is to be used in the service of the needy and is not to be viewed as an automatic entitlement for leadership in the church.

The second chapter of Kidd's monograph (1990:35–109) deals with the Greco-Roman culture of benefaction, as well as the social implications of what he aptly terms the system of "incentives and reciprocities" by which wealthy *Bürgers* were bound to their communities (1990:112). Kidd acknowledges that there are *bürgerlich* aspects of the Pastorals. The letters uphold the moral values and virtues affirmed by the wealthy, expecting them to be generous and liberal, and to use their wealth to benefit others. However, the letters are anti-*bürgerlich* as well. The writer condemns haughtiness: the rich are not to regard themselves as superior people. Immortality in the form of public honors is not the reward for benefactions bestowed upon the church. Rather, benefactors are to place their hope in heavenly rewards, not in any reciprocity from earthly "friends." In this way, the author challenges and subverts the whole fabric of the benefaction culture so significant for living as a *Bürger.* Dibelius's theory has been found seriously wanting in this aspect. The Pastoral Epistles both share and do not share some quite fundamental assumptions about wealth and civic obligation in the Greco-Roman world.

Chapter 4 (1990:159–94) tackles the claim that the ethics of the letters are "unheroically conservative." Is it true, Kidd asks, that the author has surrendered Paul's willingness to put up with the status quo because it is provisional, the end being imminent? Has the author come to accept "present inegalitarian conditions as being necessary for the church's survival in the world"?

(1990:159). Kidd insists that the author does not break with apocalyptic expectations. In fact the end is imminent: these are the "last days" (see 2 Tim 3:1–4). Paul himself regarded the church as a community of unequals. Galatians 3:28 refers not to social equality but to equal status before God. At this point, the Pastorals are consonant with Paul, Kidd contends. Like Roland Schwarz before him, he seeks to demonstrate that ethical exhortation is often predicated on the certainty of eschatological hope (1990:171, 173; cf. Schwarz 1983:104–5). While Kidd may be overly confident that the undisputed Pauline letters and the Pastorals agree on the matter of "social posture" and apocalyptic expectation, this should not detract from the insightfulness of Kidd's overall analysis. The concept of "bourgeois Christianity," as applied to the Pastorals, can no longer be maintained in the form Dibelius articulated it.

Institutionalization in the Pastoral Epistles

We have already had cause to reflect on the sense that the letters testify to a growing institutionalization in the Pauline churches after the death of the apostle. It is alleged that the Pauline communities were entirely governed by the Spirit and were wholly charismatic in their organization and ministry. A number of influential scholars in the twentieth century contrasted and underscored the contrast between the Spirit-endowed, indiscriminately bestowed ministries manifest, say, in the Corinthian church, with the concern for hierarchy and order evident in the Pastorals.

Early Catholicism

Ernst Käsemann's article "Paul and Early Catholicism" (1969:237–51) masterfully draws the contrast between charismatically endowed ministry and institutionalized ministry. He argues that the ecclesiastical polity that emerged early in the writings of the second century, including the Pastorals, was a response to the crisis stimulated by the waning of the expectation of an imminent parousia and the ferment of enthusiasm (1969:242, 247). This polity, with its stress on the cadre of official ministers over against a nonministering laity, is far from the situation perceived in the Pauline *homologoumena*. In these letters, all believers are addressed as charismatics. The later development can be characterized as "early catholic," and, as such, represents a jettisoning of the freedom of believers moved to minister by the Spirit for the safety of the routinization of ministerial office and cultic celebration.

Institutionalization in the Pauline and Post-Pauline Churches

Margaret MacDonald's important study (1988) of the stages of institutionalization of ministry and organization in the Pauline corpus provides a corrective to highly contrastive studies, such as that of Käsemann, in which developments in order and ministry are merely plotted and even lamented. She maintains that tracing the development of institutionalization in the Pauline and post-Pauline churches will result in a more complete understanding when sociological methods, not just historical ones, are employed. In this way, she is confident that we will learn more about how and why the transformations under analysis took place. She employs insights from the social sciences in order to illuminate the social world of the Pauline communities, arguing that the world of the early Pauline believers was a catalyst for change in the ministry and order of the churches.[12] Her aim is to comprehend the "dialectic relationship existing between beliefs and social structures" (1988:9).

MacDonald is particularly indebted to the sociological models, mostly derived from Weber, employed by Bengt Holmberg in *Paul and Power* (1980), a study of order in the Pauline communities. Holmberg locates the beginnings of institutionalization with Paul himself. As can be seen in his letters, Paul supports the various local offices arising naturally in the churches he addresses and values their independence. Furthermore, by engaging in dialogue with his readers, answering their questions, criticizing and exhorting them, he builds up their knowledge and capacity for discrimination and judgment. The letters are both an exercise in apostolic authority and a "diffusion" of that authority (1980:186).

MacDonald advocates a threefold, cumulative development of institutionalization in the Pauline corpus corresponding to the span of the three generations addressed. These three stages are: (1) community-building institutionalization—evident in the undisputed Pauline letters, (2) community-stabilizing institutionalization—evident in Colossians and Ephesians, and (3) community-protecting institutionalization—evident in the Pastorals. The documents of each stage in the development are examined with respect to four aspects of community life: attitudes to the world/ethics, ministry, ritual, and belief.

The Pastoral Epistles testify to the urgent need to stabilize community life in the light of severe challenges to its Pauline identity posed by false teachers and criticism of deviant behavior in the community from those outside it. The author of the letters takes the step of underscoring the authority of the official leaders, legitimating them as protectors and guardians of the symbolic universe that bestows a Pauline identity on the churches. In agreement with other scholars, such as Countryman and Verner, and more recently Kidd, MacDonald observes that these leaders are drawn exclusively from the ranks of well-to-do male householders who are socially respectable, conform to the ethical criteria affirmed by the Greco-Roman urban elites, and manifest the teaching aptitude required for leadership in the church. Only by preserving the values and order of the Greco-Roman household could the church, as the "household" of God, hope to embrace the empire.

Elders and Overseers

The nature of the relationship between the office of presbyter (Gr.: *presbyteros*) and overseer (Gr.: *episkopos*) has provoked fresh scholarly examination in recent years. For some commentators the offices are identical. Over a century ago, the great J. B. Lightfoot argued that the two terms are interchangeable designations of the one office (1885:95, 96–99, 193). The Gentile churches of Philippi (Phil 1:1), Asia Minor (Acts 20:28; 1 Tim 3:1), and Crete (Titus 1:7) had their overseers and deacons. Elders are to be found in churches of Jewish-Christian origin. Other scholars have argued that the overseer (always mentioned in the singular in the Pastorals) emanated from the circle of presbyters and took on an administrative role presiding over a college of elders. In time this developed into the ecclesiastical structure glimpsed in the Ignatian correspondence. Hanson (1982:31–38) argues that this is the situation encountered in the Pastorals. Other scholars argue that the letters testify to the juxtaposition of two different ecclesiastical constitutions—one, distinctively Pauline, comprising overseers and deacons (Phil 1:1); the other, Jewish-Christian, comprising elders. The Pastor, it is argued, favored the former. He sought to combine the two structures in such a way that would allow precedence to the Pauline.[13]

Frances Young has recently advocated the view that concentration on the early church as a household has obscured the possible influence of the synagogue and the institution of elders in Judaism on the churches of the Pastorals (1994a:99–111; 1994b:142–8).[14] Originally there were no elders in the Pauline churches. However, in time the overseer of the household church took on more of the administrative role associated in the synagogue with the synagogue administrator (Gr.: *archisynagogos*) (1994b:147). At the same time, the church was instituting its own eldership or presbyterate analogous to that of Judaism in which elders functioned as community leaders (1994a:109). Heavily influenced by Jewish and synagogue structures, the elders of the Christian communities took on the role of guardians of sacred tradition and memory. Just as the Jewish elders appointed the synagogue administrator as well as the offices of almoner and synagogue attendant, so the Pastorals testify to elders beginning to appoint one of their number as "overseer"

(= *archisynagogos*). The deacons were analogous to the almoners and attendants encountered in the synagogue. Thus the letters are further confirmation that the early Christians saw themselves as a third "race" (Gr.: *ethnos*), distinct from Jews and Gentiles, with their own community leaders (i.e., elders) functioning, albeit analogously, as elders did in Judaism (1994a:110; 1994b:148).

Rejecting proposed synagogue analogies and influences, R. Alistair Campbell poses an original thesis (1995:176–205). He argues that the Pastorals were written to legitimate the new office of the overseer (1995:196). The relationship between the older office of elder and the new overseer can be perceived in Titus, the earliest of the three letters. In 1:5 the author prescribes the appointing of elders town by town, a stipulation Campbell interprets to mean one elder for each town (1995:197). Noting that the Pastor immediately begins to set out the requirements for the overseer in 1:7, Campbell argues that this is the title to be given to each elder so appointed (1995:198). The situation in 1 Timothy presupposes the distinction in function earlier anticipated for the churches on Crete. Furthermore, in the Pastorals, Campbell sees a development of the house-church foundation of the ministries of the Pauline churches. The presbyterate, he suggests, should be seen as a collective denoting house-church leaders (1995:204). The overseer continues the work of the apostle or his delegates. The church order of the letters is a later development of what is already perceived to be the order operating in the Pauline mission.

Clearly, no consensus is emerging on this complex issue, except insofar as scholars seem less inclined to the older view that the terms *elder* and *overseer* are simply synonymous and interchangeable. Nevertheless, the social setting of the Pastorals, particularly with respect to possible synagogue influences, has generated new interest in the church order of the letters and the relationship of the offices.

Conclusion

The majority of scholars surveyed in this chapter have sought to investigate the contours of the urban social context of the Pastorals. They have reminded us that the social location of the believers exerts its own influence on the crafting of the New Testament corpus. Scholars have highlighted the shortsightedness of the scholarly methodology that is content merely to contrast the Pastorals with the undisputed letters, or trace the manner in which Pauline tradition is brought to speech, or defend the authenticity of the letters as though the addressees lived in a vacuum. Social context did play a crucial part in determining the manner in which the early writers addressed the churches. Scholars such as Margaret MacDonald, David Verner, William Countryman, and Reggie Kidd have demonstrated how much is brought to the study of the Pastorals by close attention to social context and, in MacDonald's case, the judicious use of sociological models. The contribution of Edwin Judge to this enterprise should not be underestimated. By bringing into relationship the highly structured urban social environment of the New Testament era and the New Testament documents themselves, he set in motion the modern quest to understand them in terms of their own social conditions. The Pastorals emerge as fully contingent attempts to address believers located in the Greco-Roman urban landscape.

4
The Literary Setting
of the Pastoral Epistles

What Is a Letter?

A vast corpus of letters survives from the Classical era, written by and for people of every social rank and status. At one end of the spectrum we encounter semiliterate papyrus letters from Egypt. At the other end, there are letters written by kings and princes, aristocrats, bishops, and philosophers. Artemon, the collector and publisher of Aristotle's letters, defined a letter as "half a conversation," an important observation for appreciating the function of letters in the ancient world.[1]

Modern interest in ancient letters can be first attributed to a Gustav Adolf Deissmann. At the end of the nineteenth century, he undertook to mediate the significance of the large numbers of newly discovered and published papyrus letters (inscriptions included) for the study of the New Testament. In two major works, originally published in German in 1895/97 and 1908 respectively—*Bibelstudien* (Eng. 1901) and *Licht vom Osten* (Eng. 1910)—he cast his inquiring and somewhat romantic mind over the exciting literary and epigraphic discoveries.[2] To him, this material suggested that the origins of Christianity lay with the activity of nonliterary, religious geniuses who ministered among the "lower classes."[3]

He drew an influential distinction between what he called "real" letters and "nonreal" epistles. Letters, he argued, were intended for immediate and private contexts. They were ephemeral, contingent, and particular. To him, the nonliterary papyrus letters afforded the best comparisons with the corpus of Pauline letters: They did not aim self-consciously at a literary style. Epistles, on the other hand, were artfully written for posterity and for a wide public. Deissmann classed the "catholic" letters of the New Testament—James, Peter, Jude—as epistles. He classed the ten-letter Pauline corpus, as well as 2 and 3 John, as letters. He regarded the Pastorals as epistles, without giving a reason for so doing (1901:54; 1910:238–39).

Although Deissmann's views were subjected to early criticism, it was not until the publication of Heikki Koskenniemi's influential *Studien zur Idee und Phraseologie des griechischen Briefes bis 400 n. Chr.* (1956) that a study of ancient letters together with insights from contemporary epistolary theorists was undertaken (see especially 1956:18–63). He concentrated on non-literary papyrus letters, the same corpus that had so motivated Deissmann. Koskenniemi isolated three essential characteristics of letters, which he tied closely to the theorists, especially Demetrius of Phalerum (fl. 300 B.C.E.). Observations on letter writing are included in the treatise *On Style* attributed to him.

The first of the characteristics is *philophronesis*. Letters, Demetrius maintained, are expressions of friendship and are graced with friendly compliments. The writer adopts a style that is without high rhetorical effect and retains the sense of conversation and dialogue. The second, *parousia,* focuses on letters as the projection of the personality and character of the writer, so that the letter renders him present even though physically absent. A personal tone is uppermost in a letter. The third, *homilia,* underscores the letter as a dialogue or conversation in written form.[4] Koskenniemi argued that the theorists did not draw a distinction between "nonreal" epistles and "real" letters. The writer modified his style to fit the context and the occasion. Other more recent scholars have also commented on Deissmann's thesis (Doty 1969:183–99; Stowers 1986:17–26; Murphy-O'Connor 1995:42–45).

In his *Letters in Primitive Christianity* (1973) William Doty argues that Paul was not simply "tossing off" his letters. Rather, he was writing self-consciously as an apostle, as one who was an official representative of the early Christian movement. He expected the letters to be read publicly in the meetings of the churches. Their paraenetic and didactic content were vital for securing the addressees in the faith they had embraced. Paul wrote to exhort, encourage, rebuke, and advise. In other words, the Pauline letters have "public intent" that brings them closer to "the official pronouncement than to the private letter" (1973:26). Paul writes as though he were present. The letters are substitutes for his personal presence.

Paul and the Letter Genre

Robert W. Funk's essay, "The Apostolic Parousia: Form and Significance" (1967:249–68) builds on the work of Heikki Koskenniemi. He argues persuasively that Pauline letters are manifestations of one of three strategies the apostle adopted in giving expression to what Funk identifies as the power and authority of his apostolic presence (parousia) with his congregations (1967:249). The other two were his actual, physical presence and the use of emissaries. The letters of the apostle, therefore, function as substitutes for the actual presence of the apostle in his authority and power. They are a significant witness to the sense of pastoral oversight Paul had for the congregations in his care. When he was absent from them and unable to send an emissary, his letters functioned as a means of keeping alive the "conversation" he had begun while present and to extend the relationship of friendship during his absence (1967:264). The fact that false teachers and false models of the Christian life made their presence felt in several of the congregations meant that the writing of letters as vehicles of his apostolic presence was all the more urgent.

Helmut Koester (1979:33–44) argues that the Pauline letters represent a new phenomenon in the early Christian movement. The first one written, namely, 1 Thessalonians, signals the creation of the Christian letter. Paul thus forges for himself a powerful weapon in his attempts to organize and sustain the churches he founded while physically absent from them (1979:33). The first collection of Paul's letters, Koester maintains, gave rise not only to collections of letters written in his name but also to other letters— 1 Peter, *1 Clement,* and the letters of Ignatius, Dionysius of Corinth, Irenaeus, and Cyprian. That the form and content of 1 Thessalonians is unprecedented, Koester observes, can be seen in the elaborate thanksgiving section, and the lengthy moral exhortations and eschatological instructions. Whereas letters served to extend the friendship of writer and addressee for friendship's sake, the letters of Paul became the medium by which apostle and his congregations were bound together "in the eschatological perspective of a new message" of which Paul was the herald (1979:37).

John L. White agrees. Paul was the first, he writes, to "popularize the letter as an authoritative form of communication within Christianity" (1983:435; cf. 1984:1739). White also argues that the Pauline letter was foundational for the later post-Pauline letter deposit. The pattern of invoking apostolic authority is shared by the pseudo-Pauline letters, 1 and 2 Peter, James, and Jude (cf. 2 and 3 John and the authority of the "presbyter").

In my own work, I have sought to demonstrate that the Pastorals are dependent on the Pauline letter form (Harding 1998:94–106). This is particularly so in their opening and closing formulae, which contain similar evocations in the form of preformed materials (prayers and hymns) of the liturgical context of the churches addressed. This, I believe, was an important strategy on the part of the Pastor. He intentionally sought to write letters that were recognizably Pauline in their general format and epistolary formulae. This form was best designed to actualize the apostle's teaching, as he understood it, for the addressees.

Moral Exhortation in the Greco-Roman World

Abraham Malherbe has drawn attention to the considerable similarity between the moral teaching of the early church and that encountered in the hellenistic and Greco-Roman moral philosophers (1992:267–70).[5] The tradition of moral philosophy can be traced to the late fifth century B.C.E. and early hellenistic times. During this period, Malherbe observes, it was argued that reason was the foundation of the moral life. Philosophers increasingly turned their attention to ethics in the conviction that right conduct was dependent on correct knowledge (1986b:11–12). Much of the philosophical discourse of the Greco-Roman era centered on ethics. Philosophers found a ready audience and were often invited to deliver public orations on some ethical topic. They taught from their homes or enjoyed the sponsorship of wealthy patrons. In this way, philosophical ethics penetrated many levels of society, as can be witnessed in extant letters, satires, and speeches in which the elements of ethical theory are assumed (Stowers 1984:66; Malherbe 1986b:13).

Rudolf Vetschera (1912) drew attention to two general modes of moral exhortation in the Greco-Roman world. In the first, which he termed *paraenesis* (Gr.: *parainesis*), the writer advised the addressee to pursue or, by contrast, to avoid, a certain way of life, affirming that commitment by reminding him or her of the ethical orientation the addressee has already chosen. Rhetorical devices, most often the adducing of positive and negative examples, reinforce that orientation. On the other hand, *protrepsis,* the second mode, is exhortation in which the addressee is urged to change his or her lifestyle and is usually exhorted to pursue a philosophical life commitment.

There is a large body of extant hortatory treatises. However, much of the literature of exhortation is in the form of letters, a form that lent itself to pursuing and affirming ethical stances because of its potential for intimacy. Scholars observe that many philosophers, especially in the Roman era, wrote "books" of letters, or followers collected and published the letters of their master in which his heritage was preserved (Quinn 1990:7–8; Stirewalt 1993:15). Sometimes pseudonymous letters were crafted to supplement these corpora (Stirewalt 1993:16–17). Stirewalt observes that the interest great philosophers (such as Plato, Aristotle, and Epicurus) and orators (such as Isocrates and Demosthenes) showed in letters explains why epistolary theory and style were introduced to philosophical and rhetorical schools (1993:15–17).

The rhetorical handbooks only incorporate analysis of letters at a late date (fourth century C.E.), and then only by way of supplement. There is evidence from an early date that philosophers and rhetoricians were interested in letters as a medium of persuasive discourse only a small distance removed from the practice of oratory. The epistolary handbooks evidence considerable interest in guiding writers to choose the right category, together with the appropriate style. Both the handbooks attributed to Demetrius (second century B.C.E.–third century C.E.) and Libanius (fourth century C.E.–sixth century C.E.) contain a number of brief examples of letters as models of the style appropriate to each type of letter. These handbooks, Malherbe suggests, were intended for the training of professional letter writers (1988:6–7).[6] He also reminds us that the writing of letters formed part of the regimen of the schools at the secondary and tertiary stages of education. It seems likely that early in the curriculum of secondary education the *grammaticus* prescribed letter-writing exercises. Malherbe judges most of the papyrus letters to have been written by those with education at this level. Learning the right style appropriate to a letter came later in the curriculum. Having advanced to education under a *rhetor,* whose task it was to mold orators, the student was required to write letters as part of the series of preparatory exercises. One of the later tasks of students at this stage in their rhetorical education was the writing of *prosopopoeia,* the purpose of which was to develop skill in "characterization or impersonation" (Malherbe 1988:7; 1992:283; cf. Deissmann 1901:13; Thraede 1970:23–24; Doty 1973:6–7; White 1986:189–90; Fiore 1986:108–10). The student was required to capture the character or persona of a great one from the past in epistolary form.

The Philosophical Tradition of Pastoral Care

Edwin Judge, in his article "St. Paul and Classical Society" (1972:19–36), addresses the ongoing endeavor to account for Paul, his situation in society, his mission, and his communities in Greco-Roman terms. He argues that the Pauline communities should not to be seen in the light of later ecclesiastical developments or the mystery cults. Rather, Judge proposes, Paul belongs to "a society of rigorous talk and argument about behavior and ideas" (1972:32). The content of this talk and argument would have been perceived as having more in common with Greco-Roman moral philosophy than with religion with its focus on ritual, sacrifice, and image (cf. Barton and Horsley 1981:30, 39–40).

In an earlier two-part article published in 1960 (1960b:4–15, 125–37), Judge contends that the contemporaries of early Christian communities might have perceived them as types of scholastic communities. The impression that Paul's activity would have given suggests that his contemporaries would have aptly categorized him as a sophist. Like the majority of his philosophical counterparts, Judge observes, Paul was concerned about the moral life. Furthermore, like them, he traveled, relied upon the patronage and hospitality of admirers, was an apt talker and persuader, was dedicated to his mission and intolerant of criticism.

Stanley Stowers affirms much of this interpretation (1984:59–82). He reminds us that Paul was not the street-corner preacher of popular imagination like the Cynics of his day (1984:60). The most likely physical and social circumstances in which Paul conducted his mission would have been the homes of his well-to-do patrons—common in the Greco-Roman era. Moral philosophers or teachers thus enjoyed legitimation and status. Indeed, philosophical schools were often based in homes. Epicurean groups, Stowers observes, were household-based. Men, women, and slaves met together as friends to remember the sayings of Epicurus. Plutarch turned his home into a philosophical school. Paul did not engage in the hit-and-run tactics of the Cynics who generally accosted people in public, berating them for their lifestyles and moral choices. Rather, Paul preached to form a community. The relationship between Paul and his communities was furthered by letters in which Paul maintained his role as pastoral guide. Some Cynics taught while they worked. Paul, it seems, was not averse to conducting his mission in this way. Significantly for Stowers, Paul and the Cynics both exemplified the view that message and conduct must "cohere and illustrate one another" (1984:80). There was continuity between everyday life and preaching activity. This is the kind of continuity that the Pastor seeks to inculcate in the letters for those who hold public office in the church.

Abraham J. Malherbe has built on these observations in assessing the work of Paul and the intention of the author of the Pastorals. In his *Paul and the Thessalonians: The Philosophic Tradition of Pastoral Care* (1987) and in a number of published articles brought together in the collection *Paul and the Popular Philosophers* (1989), Malherbe demonstrates that Paul was thoroughly familiar with the teaching methods of contemporary philosophers.[7] However, he adds, Paul was not a "technical philosopher" concerned about cosmology and metaphysics (1989:68). Rather, Paul was a preacher, like most philosophers of the day, who sought to reform the lives of his hearers. Paul was a "type of Hellenistic philosopher" who essentially exercised a function of pastoral care (1989:68). He made use of elements of the Greco-Roman philosophical moral tradition, maintaining his contacts with his congregations once absent from them. In his concern for communal living, Paul resembles the Epicureans of the era who were also concerned that moral exhortation had a communal focus. He presented himself to the Thessalonians like a Cynic of gentle mien pastorally committed to his addressees, and not a harsh, excoriating critic (1989:47–48).

The Pastoral Epistles are situated in this philosophical environment of pastoral care (1989:121–36, 137–45). Malherbe shows how the extensive imagery drawn from the practice of medicine and surgery evident in the letters can best be understood from contemporary philosophical discourse. Philosophers also used the language of disease and health encountered in the Pastorals to distinguish the false teachers from the sound teaching of the socially responsible teachers. The harsh variety of Cynic was particularly polemicized against in this fashion, as Lucian and Dio Chrysostom demonstrate. The Pastor frequently indulges in polemic of this order. In contrast to the diseased mind and motives of the false teachers, the faithful teacher will teach what will promote the moral progress of the believers and will enhance social stability, knowing when to rebuke and when to affirm those in his care. Timothy and Titus emulate Paul in this regard. Nevertheless, paradoxically, 2 Timothy 4:2 demonstrates that Timothy maintains a harsh Cynic attitude toward the false teachers, not at all cultivating the ability to choose the right time when to offer rebuke (1989:143). Malherbe concludes that, according to the Pastor, the opponents are beyond reformation and hope of cure.

In his valuable study of letter writing, Stanley Stowers (1986) remarks how early Christian writers, Paul included, used letters to form the character of the congregations to whom they wrote (1986:42–43). We have seen above that letters were regarded as particularly apt vehicles for the projection of the character of the writer. Acknowledging his debt to Malherbe's article " 'Gentle as a Nurse' " (1989:35–48), Stowers argues that Paul and other letter writers were participating in a venerable tradition observed among philosophers and their protégés. Letters passing between philosopher-psychagogue and protégé were the principal medium of instruction and exhortation in the philosophical life. In the letters of the New Testament, of which Paul's is the most extensive collection, the building of the character of the community is seen as something superintended by the power of God revealed in Christ. Nevertheless, Paul appears something of a psychagogue in his letters, exhorting by way of reminder, carrying on a catechetical ministry, advising, rebuking, and settling disputes. In agreement with Malherbe, Stowers observes that the Epicureans present the closest analogy to the kind of letter-writing, character-building movement that characterizes Paul's literary relationship with his churches.[8]

In the post-Pauline era, followers of Paul, perhaps members of his retinue, carried on another tradition also seen among philosophical groups: the writing of pseudonymous letters in the name of an esteemed master for purposes of moral exhortation. In the Pastorals, Stowers argues, Paul is presented as the "model of the bold but gentle teacher and community builder" (1986:43). The false teachers, on the other hand, are vilified. In contrast to Paul, they provide a set of contrasting negative hortatory models. The letters also continue the tradition of Paul as philosophical psychagogue. The Pastor wrote in Paul's name to trusted associates, indeed former emissaries (see 1 Cor 4:16–17; 16:10–11; 1 Thess 3:2; Phil 2:19–22 [Timothy]; 2 Cor 8:6, 17, 23 [Titus]). He wrote with the same intention as the apostle. He sought to mold Christian character and called for sustained defense of the apostolic deposit—the Pauline heritage—that perpetuated a dynamic thrust and identity to the communal life of the post-Pauline churches addressed.

The Pastoral Epistles as Letters of Moral Exhortation

Stowers, Malherbe, and Judge have argued that Paul saw himself and was perceived by his contemporaries as a type of moral philosopher engaged in the practice of psychagogy or pastoral care. The Pastorals continue and enhance this picture of Paul. Paul is an example to be emulated and the guarantor of sound teaching, writing to former emissaries to defend his heritage and to implacably oppose the false teachers. The polemic of the letters, as Malherbe as shown, is redolent of that encountered among the philosophers (1989:123–27; cf. Karris 1971:1–44; 1972:549–64).

Stowers (1986:91–152) extensively discusses the category of letters of exhortation and advice, believing it to be the most frequently encountered in the New Testament (1986:96–97). He argues that the Pastorals might be compared to letters of this category, singling out Pliny the Younger's letter to Maximus (*Epistles* viii.24) as a parallel (1986:103–4). Maximus, Pliny's junior, is about to assume the post of imperial legate in Achaea, and paraenetic letters were often written on the occasion of such undertakings. The analogy with the Pastorals, in which Timothy and Titus are exhorted to persevere in their respective undertakings, is clear.

Benjamin Fiore's fine monograph, *The Function of Personal Example in the Socratic and Pastoral Epistles* (1986), is an extensive literary-critical analysis of the rhetorical use of personal example in these two corpora. He begins by noting the inadequacy of approaches to the Pastorals that do not do justice to their literary form and genre as of first importance. He places the letters squarely in the venerable tradition of literary hortatory discourse, especially as exemplified in the epistolary deposit. The letters are further characterized by reproof, correction, and admonition, and by emphasis on the need for right instruction and teaching—traits characteristic of the paraenetic tradition. Further underscoring their hortatory nature, Fiore notes the frequency of imperative verbs, the virtue and vice lists, the vocative address, and the use of exclamation, hyperbole, and gnomic sayings. Moreover, the addressees are exhorted by way of reminder and in accord with the values of conventional wisdom. Fiore also argues that the loose structure of each of the letters is analogous to hortatory discourses, observing, however, that "the tension of opposites" in the presentation of contrasting examples provides what overall structure there is in the letters (1986:21).

Fiore locates the literary precedents of the paraenetical character of the Pastorals in the long tradition of literary moral exhortation of the hellenistic world, which, in turn rests on earlier oral discourse and the rhetorical craft. Even though they are ostensibly orations, the kingship treatises of Plutarch and Dio Chrysostom, as well as treatises attributed to Isocrates (namely, *To Demonicus* and *To Nicocles*), furnish excellent parallels of the style and occasion of the Pastorals (1986:78; cf. Spicq 1969:1.38–39). The subject of these treatises and the persuasive devices used found their way into the letters of the period, chiefly in letters of philosophers, such as those of Seneca and the pseudonymous Socratic Letters. The latter date from the early empire and are preserved in the collection of Cynic Epistles (1986:85). The collection uses example as a persuasive technique in ways that recall its use in the Pastorals. The collection also comprises different letter types, thus diversifying the rhetorical effect and appeal of the corpus. This characteristic is shared on a smaller scale with the Pastorals, which are comprised of two paraenetic letters (1 Timothy and Titus) and a testament in letter form (2 Timothy).

The purpose of the Socratic letters also bears comparison with the Pastorals. The former were written in a rhetorically informed manner to preserve and promote what the author understands to be the authentic teaching of Socrates in the face of aberrant forms of it (1986:194). The author seeks to urge his audience to subscribe to the "mild" Cynicism now seen as the vehicle of Socrates' teaching and way of life. In a similar fashion, the Pastorals actualize the virtue and way of life of the apostle Paul for the purpose of urging the audience to follow his moral example. The personalia, often regarded as marks of the authenticity of the letters, serve to underscore the character of the apostle and to underscore the contrast with the false teachers. They appear in the Socratic deposit with similar intent (1986:227–28). Subscribing to the false teachers, who are perceived by Fiore as foils for the one sound teacher, constitutes the wrong choice (1986:195–96; cf. Karris 1972:563; Johnson 1978–79:1-26; Donelson 1986:92).

The concern of the letters, Fiore concludes, is to establish well-ordered communities with sound, responsible leaders, who are faithful to the principles of their founding father (1986:229).

2 Timothy and the Testament Genre

Benjamin Fiore is one of a number of recent scholars who note that the Pastorals are actually a collection of letters of two broad types, namely, paraenetic (1 Timothy and Titus) and testamentary (2 Timothy). John J. Collins defines the testament genre as a "discourse delivered in anticipation of imminent death" (1984:325). He observes that testaments so defined exist in the Hebrew Bible, the early Jewish corpus, and in Greek philosophical literature.

For Collins, the three defining characteristics of the genre are exemplified in the *Testaments of the Twelve Patriarchs (T12P)*. These characteristics are (1) historical retrospective reviewing the testator's life, (2) ethical exhortation, and (3) prediction of the future (1984:325). Although only a few works of the era are rightly classed as testaments, testamentary features are found embedded in works of other genres such as Tobit (14), 1 Maccabees (2:49–70), and Jubilees (21, 36). In the New Testament, John 13—17 and Acts 20:18–35 are testamentary.

Eckhard von Nordheim classifies testaments as wisdom literature (1980:1.229–42). Moral exhortation is the writers' aim. He observes that in the Jewish testaments, exhortation is usually directed toward inculcating faithfulness to the law and singling out the dangers of idolatry and sexual sins. The review of the testator's life and prediction of the future are subservient vehicles for exhortation. The testator functions as a powerful moral example, his life furnishing positive and negative examples for the audience.

Although Klaus Berger observes that characteristics of the testament genre are scattered through 2 Timothy, which, after all, is a letter, his analysis of the genre highlights a significant aspect for the study of 2 Timothy (1984:75–80). He argues that Jewish testaments are closely allied to the concept of tradition and, consequently, make provision for the transmission of the testator's teaching and moral exhortation. He posits the *Testament of Simeon* (of the *T12P*) as an example of this concern. The patriarch exhorts his children to be obedient to Levi and Judah because God will raise up a high priest and a savior king from them, respectively (see *T. Sim.* 7.2). He adds: "For this reason I command these things to you and you command them to your children, so that they may observe them in their successive generations" (*T. Sim.* 7.3 [cf. *T. Levi* 10.1]).

Here the Greek word translated as "observe" is that used in the Pastorals for the "guarding" of the Pauline heritage. Michael Wolter also highlights this aspect of 2 Timothy (1988:222–41). In his discussion of the relationship of 2 Timothy to the testament genre, he observes how significant is the need in the letters for the preservation of the Pauline tradition through the careful choice of successors of the apostolic delegates (see 2 Tim 2:2).

I have endeavored to demonstrate that 2 Timothy, though in letter form, is essentially testamentary in its content (Harding 1998:150–53). In light of his impending death, Paul, as "father," takes his leave of his "son," Timothy. He reminds him of the responsibility to guard the heritage with which he has been entrusted, and to which the three letters as a corpus have given voice. Like a spiritual director, Paul exhorts Timothy to persevere in the ministry to which he has been called. Paul poses as an ethical paradigm, a faithful witness who has stayed the course, one who is unrelentingly devoted to the ministry of the gospel. Paul predicts that false teachers will come (3:1–9), and that many will fall away (1:15; 2:17–18; 4:10). Timothy, by contrast, is to persevere in what he has learned. The Pastor thus mounts a potent strategy of moral exhortation, combining the sanction accorded "last words" with the authority and persuasive dynamic of the apostle to which all three letters testify.

Seán Charles Martin (1997) also argues that the Pastor employed the form of the testament in crafting 2 Timothy, the last of the Pastorals to be written. The Pastor presents Paul in Mosaic terms.[9] The bulk of the monograph is devoted to surveys of the last words of Moses in Deuteronomy 31—34 and in early Judaism, specifically, Philo (*Life of Moses,* 2.288–92), Josephus (*Antiquities,* 4.177–93, 312–14, 320–31), Pseudo-Philo (*Biblical Antiquities,* 19.1–16), and the *Testament of Moses.* Deuteronomy 31—34, he observes, is foundational for all subsequent farewell discourses in the Jewish tradition. The Pastor brings Paul back from the dead, as it were, and has him speak again, definitively, to another generation that was facing a crisis in authority (1997:15). The apostolic witnesses had died. The churches, specifically those to whom the Pastorals were written, are presented with the problem of identifying the legitimate successors of the apostle Paul. The Pastor wrote to protect the Pauline heritage and to set before the believers the authority of Paul, as another Moses, whose wishes as a faithful minister at the point of death are recorded in the testamentary letter that is 2 Timothy.

While Martin's arguments for the very specific Mosaic cast of the presentation of Paul seem strained at points, there is no doubt that he is correct in identifying the rhetorical potency of 2 Timothy as the testament of Paul. Regarding the emotional power of the presentation of Paul as the undaunted, faithful minister who is about to die, Martin is surely right to invoke the canons of rhetorical discourse. As a testament, the letter, when taken with 1 Timothy and Titus, bestows a "well-nigh unimpeachable" authority to the prescriptions and vision of church life encapsulated in all three letters (1997:230).

Jerome Quinn agrees. In his article "Parenesis and the Pastoral Epistles" (1981:495–501), he aptly captures the power of 2 Timothy and the Pastorals as a whole, when he characterizes 2 Timothy as a will, the last words of the apostle to his "legitimate child." The paraenesis of 2 Timothy, he argues, is thereby invested with an "irrefutable, incontestable character." It will admit of no refutation (1981:499).

Conclusion

Investigating the Pastorals in a way that takes seriously the literary embodiment of the Pastor's message is an integral aspect of understanding them as documents of early Christianity. This enterprise is just as significant as the investigation of the thought world and social context of the letters, and rightly coheres with that task. The letters evoke a significant aspect of Paul's pastoral guidance of the churches he founded, namely, his apostolic presence mediated through the vehicle of the letter genre. We have also seen how the Pastorals, together with the other letters of the Pauline corpus, belong to the tradition of pastoral care as undertaken by philosophers with their students and protégés. The letters are seen to belong to the tradition of writing letters of moral exhortation. The function of Paul as a powerful moral example has also been underscored.

In the next chapter, our focus turns to the rhetoric of the letters, already anticipated in this chapter. Moral exhortation depends for its effectiveness on strategies of persuasion. Though the writing of letters might be a familiar, even perfunctory, exercise for us, for the Pastor it was the most primary and foundational of the persuasive strategies he employs. That he should write letters in Paul's name means that he was seeking to actualize the esteemed Paul of memory who wrote letters as extensions of his apostolic brief. By writing letters in Paul's name, he signals his intention to engage his hearers on matters of supreme salvific importance and to elicit from them assent to his vision of the Pauline legacy.

5
The Pastoral Epistles and Classical Rhetoric

Introduction

The spoken word dominated public life in Classical Greece and the Greco-Roman world. To be able to speak well, that is, persuasively, was essential in political and judicial life. The highest education possible was conducted by a *rhetor* who prepared young men for life in the public arena by teaching the techniques and craft of oratory. Rhetorical handbooks and theoretical treatments from the fourth century B.C.E. to late Roman times are an eloquent testimony both to the persistence of interest in the medium of oral, public discourse and the standardization of rhetorical theory throughout the millennium.

George Kennedy has done more than any other contemporary scholar to demonstrate the fruitfulness of analyzing the New Testament from the perspective of Classical and Greco-Roman rhetorical theory and practice. Since the 1960s, he has published a number of monographs devoted to the study of the rhetorical tradition from Classical times to the era of the New Testament and the early church down to the modern era. Kennedy concludes one of his books with the observation that "[c]lassical rhetoric was one of the constraints under which New Testament writers worked" (1984:160). To read the New Testament without this awareness is to invite and to perpetuate lack of clarity in interpretation. Kennedy's enterprise has proven to be a catalyst for an increasingly voluminous publication of books and articles focusing on aspects of the rhetoric of the New Testament. Although he notes Paul's ostensible eschewal of rhetorical craft (see 1 Cor 2:1–5; 2 Cor 11:6), he argues that the apostle was familiar with rhetorical conventions as used by lawyers, philosophers, and letter writers (1999:149). The Pastorals have been little exposed to the analysis of rhetorical critics. Nevertheless, in this chapter we will survey some significant investigations.

Letters are not speeches. Speeches were highly structured and stylistically ornamented. Theoretically, they were to be crafted according to set patterns. But exhortatory letters aimed at advice, and letters are sufficiently close to oral discourse as to invite the use of techniques of argumentation that were employed by orators. These techniques were displayed in public and were often imitated and satirized. Because of their use by philosophers and orators, such as Plato, Isocrates, and Epicurus, letters became part of the educational curriculum that aimed to produce orators (Stirewalt 1993:15–17). However, as we saw in the previous chapter, the first extant rhetorical handbook on letter writing was that of Julius Victor (fourth century C.E.). The reason for this is that letters did not use the highly stylized and inventive techniques appropriate to speeches. However, scholars rightly perceive that the techniques of rhetoric were sufficiently akin to the requirements of literary medium of letters that they attached themselves to it.[1] Moreover, much of the theoretical discussion of rhetoric is concerned with the art of persuasion per se, and is applicable to any medium that has persuasive intent (cf. Young 1992:115).

The "Species" of Rhetoric

The rhetorical theorists speak of three categories, or "species," of rhetoric. Each corresponds to a rhetorical situation. Apologetic (sometimes termed *forensic* or *judicial*) oratory was appropriate to the law court in defending a client or accusing a defendant. Deliberative oratory was crafted for use in the public assembly for exhorting and dissuading with respect to a course of action under consideration. The species of rhetoric appropriate to public occasions, such as a funeral, victory, or a commemoration, was termed epideictic. This is the oratory of display, the speaker seeking to apportion praise or censure (see Burgess 1902:82–253). The recommended arrangement of speeches, especially in the first of the two species, is similar. The attention of the audience is engaged in a *proemium* or *exordium,* a statement of the case is provided in the *narratio,* proofs are offered and anticipated objections met in the *confirmatio,* and the orator sums up the argument in a *conclusio* or *peroratio.*

Stanley Stowers notes the interconnection of rhetorical theory and the craft of letter writing (1986:51–56). There are types of letters, he argues, that correspond to the three species of rhetoric, though some defy easy classification (1986:51). Just as there were judicial speeches so there were judicial letters. The analogy holds for deliberative letters as well as those of praise and blame. Nevertheless, Stowers acknowledges, the correspondence works only partially. Letters were not integrated into rhetorical theory and many of the types encountered in the epistolary theorists are modes of exhortation or paraenesis. These were "only tangentially related to rhetorical theory," belonging more to the realm of moral philosophy (1986:52). Significantly, Stowers implies that the theory and practice of rhetoric reflected cultural values that pervaded the Classical and Greco-Roman eras. These values, which were largely concerned with honor and shame, are brought to speech in oratory and letters alike and determine the argumentative strategies employed by practitioners in all areas of educated public discourse and communication (1986:25–31).

Jerome Murphy-O'Connor (1995:65–86) concurs with this position. He notes that letters are substitutes for speech. In common with John White and other scholars, he agrees that rhetorical techniques had an influence on letter writing. Murphy-O'Connor makes the point that the theory encountered in the rhetorical handbooks never quite matches the practice, and that a mixture of the species of rhetoric can be found in the one speech. While a number of Paul's letters can be classified according to the species, the Pastorals cannot be considered speeches since they are "formally addressed to individuals." Thus they escape rhetorical classification (1995:71). He also warns of the dangers of taking a rhetorical schema and applying it to letters or parts of them, detecting in some scholars an inflexible forcing of the text into schematic shackles.

R. Dean Anderson, Jr. (1996) offers a similar caveat. Letters cannot be forced into any one of the three rhetorical species (1996:109). Such attempts, he insists, are vain. Is it legitimate, Anderson asks, to apply rhetorical genres from the arena of the spoken word to letters? Nevertheless, he acknowledges that rhetorical methods and argumentation may have influenced Paul "more generally" (1996:109). Few scholars, I suspect, would disagree.[2]

It would be misguided, I believe, to search for evidence of a rhetorical schema in any of the Pastoral Epistles. However, there is reason enough to associate the letters with the rhetorical tradition with respect to argumentative and persuasive intent. The pervasiveness of oratory as the vehicle par excellence for the public articulation and affirmation of cultural values means that no educated discourse, including letter writing, in the Greco-Roman world could be isolated from its influence. Despite the disclaimer that he was "untrained in rhetoric" (2 Cor 11:6), Paul was sufficiently familiar with rhetorical conventions to mount a parody of them in 2 Corinthians 11:22–33.[3] In fact, scholars have detected considerable use of rhetorical technique in the Pauline corpus. Attempts to show Paul in command of the conventions of the organization of a speech in his letters are more controversial. In my own book I have attempted to show that, as letters that feature moral exhortation in the form of advice from a superior to an inferior, the Pastorals are to be allied in a general sense with the deliberative species of rhetoric. Aristotle himself links ethics and rhetoric.[4] The Pastorals are also epideictic in mood to the extent that they invite praise of Paul and censure of the false teachers. This means no more than one can expect the writer to present his message in ways that evoke the persuasive strategies of speeches. The rhetorical schema that enables identification with a particular species of rhetoric may not be present, but scholars rightly detect considerable indebtedness in the Pastorals to the persuasive strategies recommended in the rhetorical handbooks and observed in speeches of the Classical and Greco-Roman eras.

Strategies of Argumentation

Recently scholars have been observing that persuasive argumentation in the New Testament is often constructed according to what George Kennedy terms the three modes of "artistic proof" (Kennedy 1984:14–16). Generally, these are arguments that appeal to reason *(logos),* or are grounded in the trustworthy character of the speaker *(ethos),* or are arguments that appeal to the emotions of the audience *(pathos).* The survey below of scholars investigating the argumentative strategies of the Pastoral Epistles highlights the use of the "proofs" by the Pastor.

Lewis Donelson on Enthymemes and Paradigms

In contrast to a number of highly negative and even dismissive readings of the theology of the Pastorals, Lewis Donelson (1986) observes that scholars have recently detected evidence of a distinctive theological system in the letters that is not dependent on Paul or Pauline tradition but points to creativity on the part of the Pastor. However, these scholars have not investigated the possibility that behind the disparate materials comprising the letters there might be a coherent argumentative strategy. Even defenders of the authenticity of the Pastorals have examined each of the various kinds of material in the letters in isolation. Donelson embarks on the ambitious project of incorporating all the diverse materials of the three letters and the forms of argumentation employed by the author "into one hermeneutical point of view" (1986:2).

While there is no logical movement from one topic to the next in the Pastorals, there is a systematic means by which one can comprehend their argumentative strategies. Donelson argues that the Pastor "create[s] logical interdependencies" within each topic addressed (1986:3). The author uses two commonly recommended modes of argument, both discussed by Aristotle: syllogistically framed rhetorical deductions (enthymemes), and both inductive and illustrative paradigms. In his *Art of Rhetoric,* Aristotle advised the use of enthymemes in which one of the elements of the syllogism was suppressed, arguing that it was not persuasive to state the obvious. The audience completes the argument. Donelson perceives that the Pastor is using this strategy in his letters. 2 Timothy 3:17, for example, contains an enthymeme on the pedagogical value of scripture. On his analysis, the minor premise is "scripture equips one for good works"; the result clause is "therefore, study scripture." The major premise—"a man of God should do good works"—is suppressed (1986:74).

The Pastor frames his deductive arguments in accord with his belief system. The persuasive force of the arguments thus devised would be effective only among those who shared the presuppositions of the author. Donelson argues that the Pastor derives his enthymemes from three fields—salvation statements, the character of the Christian life, and the "entrusted traditions." The author writes in such a way that the presuppositions of the audience are repeatedly affirmed and underscored in the interests of protecting the ecclesiastical vision of author and addressees now under attack from false teachers. In effect, the author is arguing about what leads to salvation and what does not (1986:81). He does this, Donelson shows, in a rhetorically literate manner.

The Pastor also uses paradigms effectively. For example, he presents Paul as the prototype of the Christian leader and the exemplar of Christian virtue. The opponents, on the other hand, illustrate the "contrary principles" of the Christian life (1986:92). Two contrasting lifestyles are played off against each other. One, exemplified by the false teachers, leads to judgment and eschatological condemnation. Paul, Timothy, Titus, and the teachers who succeed them are mediators of a plan of salvation first brought to life in Christ. Conformity of life to the entrusted traditions Paul has bequeathed to Timothy and Titus, and which they, in turn, have passed on to faithful men, constitutes the one lifestyle that leads (with the empowerment of the Holy Spirit bestowed in baptism) to eternal life. Church leaders who behave properly become, in Donelson's words, "the essential element in realizing salvation in the author's day" (1986:138).

Thus the Pastorals are not composed merely of disparate and eclectic materials but are analogous to the diatribal teaching methods of Epictetus and other ethicists in which diversity and variety of topics are perceived as essential means of persuasion (1986:111). Moreover—and this is Donelson's major contribution to the understanding of the letters—the author possesses a coherent theology allied to an argumentative strategy in which enthymemes link theological propositions to ethical conclusions, and paradigms are the vehicles for a powerful presentation of contrasting ethical lifestyles. As we saw in Chapter 1, James Miller, in *The Pastoral Epistles as Composite Documents,* is the latest proponent of the opposite point of view. Miller only engages Donelson as an afterthought, confining his assessment to a few pages in an appendix (1997:159–67). He admits the force of the Donelson's thesis regarding the organization of "small groups of sentences which belong structurally together" (1997:167), but remains unpersuaded by the general thrust of the book. The fact that Donelson assumes that the Pastorals are pseudonymous seems unjustifiable in the light of Miller's contention that there are genuine Pauline fragments embedded in them. Nevertheless, I believe Donelson has mounted a particularly effective counter to the tradition of scholarship that has persistently presented the

Pastor as an artless compiler and the letters as a farrago of disparate materials.

Moral Example

Arguments grounded in the character of Paul and the opponents are effective rhetorical strategies used by the Pastor. Several scholars have sought to illuminate the force of these. As we saw in the previous chapter, Benjamin Fiore (1986) has helpfully analyzed the use of moral examples—both positive and negative—in the letters. Moral philosophers and rhetoricians alike recognize the rhetorical force of these. Fiore argues that the personalia of 2 Timothy 4:6–22 and Titus 3:12–15 present Paul as the model of the selfless, self-sacrificing pastor whose life and death are marked by contentment and perseverance in the work God has called him to do. In the midst of suffering and abandonment, he faithfully maintains his apostolic brief in the unconducive context of prison. Thus the Pastor sets out examples for the audience, the leaders in particular, to emulate. John T. Fitzgerald (1988) takes this a step further in his study of the hardship catalogues of 1 Corinthians 4:9–13, 2 Corinthians 4:8–9 and 6:4–10. Fitzgerald contends that these catalogues are modeled on similar presentations in Greco-Roman philosophical literature in which the suffering of the sage serves to "magnify him as a person and establish him as a reliable guide for those who aspire to the life of virtue" (1988:203). Paul intentionally casts himself as a sage—an embodiment of reason and virtue. The catalogues thus function as a "litmus test of character." They are a rhetorical device for "distinguishing true philosophers from false ones" (1988:203, 206; cf. Epictetus, *Discourses* 2.19–24). As Fitzgerald acknowledges in several footnotes, his conclusions could be applied to the portrait of Paul in the Pastorals (1988:47 n.4; 167 n.141). I believe the Pastor evokes the idea of the worthy sage—Socrates comes most readily to mind—in his portrayal of Paul. The apostle faces death calmly, without bitterness or threat, in full assurance that his reward is in heaven and that he has run the race God has set before him.

Polemic

As Donelson and Fiore have argued, the Pastor uses the contrasting paradigms of Paul and the false teachers to fashion effective arguments the persuasive force of which is dependent upon the audience's prior allegiance to Paul as their apostle. The sustained polemic directed against the false teachers has attracted the attention of a number of recent scholars. In his 1971 Harvard dissertation and a subsequent article (1972:549–64), Robert J. Karris notes the considerable indebtedness of the Pastor to the technique of vilification used by philosophers against the sophists. This consists of recognizably stock denunciations of their greed and deception, their failure to practice what they preach, their indulgence in verbal quibbling, and their predilection for subverting women (cf. Dibelius-Conzelmann 1972:21; Karris 1971:1–44). All these are present in the Pastor's polemic against the false teachers. However, Karris observes that some charges brought against the false teachers are sufficiently nontraditional that they provide some insight into their identity. Consequently, he affirms the Jewish cast of their teaching and argues that they teach asceticism with respect to foods and marriage. Their teaching that the resurrection has already happened (see 2 Tim 2:17–18) is also distinctive. It is also clear that the false teachers encourage emancipationist ideals with respect to women and slaves (see 1 Tim 2:11–15, 6:3; cf. Karris 1972:552–55). In this respect and in the light of early Jewish and Christian speculation that Eve was sexually seduced by the serpent in the Garden, it is difficult to imagine a more powerful indictment of the practice of women teaching men than that presented in 1 Timothy 2:11–15.[5] The Pastor argues that by nature women lack the necessary self-control and self-mastery of which men alone are capable. Being a submissive childbearer is a woman's appropriate station in life—one that holds out the promise of salvation.

The polemic serves a rhetorical purpose. Karris argues that the author regards his teaching as the one true philosophy: that of the opponents is false. The polemic directed against the false teachers creates aversion to their interpretation of the Pauline heritage (1972:563). On the other hand, the virtue lists of the Pastorals (1 Tim 3:2–3, 8; Titus 1:7–8; 3:1–2) further contrast the false teachers with the true custodians of the Pauline tradition and guardians of the "deposit." The example of their lives will vindicate the truth of their teaching. Inasmuch as the believers in general orient their lives in accord with the teaching of the Pastorals, they will find their character and moral integrity completely and publicly vindicated. Luke Timothy Johnson (1978–79:1–26) adds his support to Karris's conclusions. By means of traditional invective, the Pastor seeks to create deep aversion to the opponents, scoring their methods and subversive teaching. By contrast, he praises Paul and the pastors who are committed to his teaching. From the beginning of his literary enterprise he proceeds, with starkly drawn comparisons, to mark out the boundaries of life in accordance with faith and saving truth from life that accords with deceit and eschatological shipwreck.

Pathos

Arguments designed to appeal to the emotions of the audience are frequently encountered in the New Testament, not least in the Pastorals, 2 Timothy especially. As we saw in the previous chapter, 2 Timothy has pronounced testamentary features. The letter, as has been often observed, encapsulates Paul's last words. False colleagues have forsaken him. He is in physical danger. He daily faces death. He is a transparently good man, a sage whose impending death, while thoroughly undeserved, is faced with calmness and without bitterness. In such circumstances the worth and character of the apostle shine forth clearly. His suffering is the ultimate sanction for and ground of his mandates for life in the church that leads to salvation.

As we saw at the end of the previous chapter, Seán Martin (1997) and Jerome Quinn (1981:495–501) both argue that the Pastor's choice of the testament in which to cast the message of 2 Timothy exerts a powerful rhetorical influence on the message of the three letters as a whole. Paul speaks definitively, finally, irrevocably. No refutation of his mandates or his vision can be admitted.

The Pastor and His Audience

In his *Art of Rhetoric,* Aristotle contends that not only must the persuasive speaker appear to be a certain type of person (if only for the sake of the effectiveness of arguments based on his ethos), he must put his audience in a frame of mind whereby it will be favorably disposed toward his cause. Failure to establish good will and rapport will result in the failure of the intent of the speech. In book 2.2–11 Aristotle embarks on a lengthy analysis of the various kinds of audience an orator might address and the appropriate disposition he commends him to adopt in each case to create that good will more effectively, from the beginning of the speech to its conclusion.

In my book, I have sought to demonstrate that the Pastor wrote "cohesively," to use George B. Caird's term, creating a "sense of mutual trust and common ethos" (1980:32). Caird observes that beyond small talk, biblical authors also appeal to common traditions and other authorities revered in common, as well as the language of worship, to establish rapport. In this enterprise it was essential for the Pastor as a pseudepigrapher to expend considerable care in the service of the larger cause of affirming and commending the Pauline heritage as he interpreted it against the inroads of custodians of the heritage he considered false and deceptive. Creating a disposition of good will helps to ensure that his urgent message will be accepted as Paul's.

I argue that the Pastor achieves good will by his use of four types of material (Harding 1998:192–93). First, the "faithful sayings" scattered through 1 Timothy and Titus are authoritative pronouncements, part of the Pauline heritage. They are known and esteemed by the audience. The Pastor uses these to affirm the ethical teaching he imparts. Second, the Pastor and his audience share a commitment to the same moral ideals and social conventions. These are articulated throughout the letters. Where there is the potential for disagreement, he invokes the supreme authority of Paul to settle the issue. Third, the literary conventions of the Pauline letter are reproduced in the Pastorals. The letters' greeting formulae, their personalia, their evocation of the apostolic parousia and the evidences of apostolic pastoral care all commend the letters as Pauline communications. Fourth, the Pastor cites liturgical and hymnic materials presumably known to the audience.

Conclusion

The Pastoral Epistles are not speeches. They are letters that fit the broad category of letters of moral exhortation. However, the opportunity to investigate them in the light of rhetorical theory shows that the Pastor uses persuasive techniques commended in the handbooks and demonstrated in the extant speeches of the era. A number of scholars, including myself, conclude that the Pastor wrote literately and persuasively when assessed by the rhetorical conventions of the day, thus enhancing the effectiveness of his appeal to his audience.

More than any other contemporary scholar, Lewis Donelson has demonstrated the Pastor's indebtedness to the method of rhetorical argument commended by Aristotle, the first great exponent of the theory of rhetoric. In so doing, Donelson has brought fresh insight to the study of the Pastor as a theologian and to his letters as coherent actualizations of the Pauline heritage. The author's use of positive and negative examples can also be assessed from the rhetorical point of view. In accord with the rhetoric of praise and blame, the Pastor creates a powerful image, on the one hand, of the suffering and worthy apostle and, on the other, of the utter deviousness and depravity of the false teachers. Paul is the paradigm of all faithful ministers and of the holy life that leads to eschatological felicity. The false teachers tend a perverted Pauline legacy that leads to eschatological catastrophe. In Paul's name, the Pastor seeks the audience's unqualified endorsement of his vision of ecclesiastical life. This endorsement, the Pastor knows, will only be forthcoming insofar as the audience recognizes and assents to the persona of Paul he brings to speech in his letters. That the audience, and, in time, the early church, was disposed to accept the letters as Paul's is the proof that the Pastor succeeded in creating the rapport that was essential for the audience's assent to his articulation of the Pauline legacy. Without this assent, the Pastorals would have been consigned to posterity as doubtful forgeries of no canonical worth (Donelson 1986:55; cf. Harding 1998:230–35).

6
The Meaning of the Pastoral Epistles Today

Introduction

The preceding chapters have shown that there is no shortage of stimulating scholarly discussion of the Pastorals. They have commanded the attention of scholars interested in New Testament language, the occasion of the Pauline letters, the essential concerns of Paul's theology, and the way in which the Pauline heritage was expressed by Paul's earliest interpreters. To historians, the letters are redolent with insights into the elusive social world behind the text. Those interested in the genre of New Testament letter have found the Pastorals to be vital witnesses in the development of a tradition of Christian moral exhortation. Study of Classical and Greco-Roman rhetoric has begun to demonstrate the way in which the Pastor crafted his letters for maximum persuasive effect. However, so far we have only infrequently considered issues related to their contemporary significance. The following presentation surveys the views of a number of scholars who are broadly representative of recent approaches to the letters.

Anthony T. Hanson

As we saw in Chapter 1, many scholars virtually dismiss the letters as a lamentable "fall" from Paul. According to this view, the letters testify to a spirit of acculturation and accommodation with the culturally distinctive values of the Greco-Roman urban world. Anthony T. Hanson espouses a similar viewpoint in "The Significance of the Pastoral Epistles" (1968:110–20), the thrust of which he briefly reprised in his 1982 commentary (1982:48–51). The Pastor, he concludes, "falls far short of Paul in almost every respect" (1982:50). Yet, he argues, it is difficult to see how the church would have survived if it had not moved toward an ordained ministry, prescriptive "legalism" in ethics, authoritarian methods of governing the church, and fixed forms of worship (1968:116). Had the author not defended the church against proto-Gnostic teachers, their influence would have proven "fatal" in a couple of centuries. Indeed, in stressing the universal love of God for all, the Pastor presses beyond Paul, preoccupied as he was with the relationship between Jew and Gentile. The Pastorals are to be seen as early second-century attempts to tackle problems with "vigour and success" (1982:51). Their contemporary significance, however, appears to be limited, especially if they are esteemed for what they claim to be instead of for what they are.

Philip Towner

At the conclusion of *The Goal of Our Instruction* (1989:256–57), Philip Towner reflects on the implications and significance of his study of the paraenesis of the letters. The exhortations to women and slaves, who were subscribing to the emancipationist teaching of the false teachers inspired by Galatians 3:28 (1989:248), raise important contemporary issues regarding evangelism and social action. Social institutions are to be respected even if that means curtailing for the time being the movement toward freedom. This is done to enhance the prospects for evangelism. Unruly and revolutionary behavior will only bring the enterprise to naught. In the Greco-Roman context of the Pastorals, the household, as the key societal institution, becomes the vehicle for mission. The church should move along social avenues, as far as possible according to society's conventions and rules and "ability to cope with such change" (1989:256). This brings to mind the letters' teaching on godly living. Towner reminds his readers that evangelism and "propriety of behaviour" are indissolubly linked.

Regarding the role of women in the church today, the "resolution of the matter," Towner contends, is tied up with the "broader question" of how the church relates to the surrounding structures of the "host society" (1989:257). It is clear from the New Testament that, for Paul and the writings attributed to him, the early church was not willing to sacrifice its mission "for the sake of *untimely* [author's italics] expressions of freedom" (1989:257). Yet, the church has shown itself unwilling to allow human cultural proclivities to impede it in the realization of salvation, a prospect, which Towner implies, assuredly involves the removal of all that perpetuates divisions—whether based on cultural, gender, or racial grounds—in accord with Galatians 3:28. In the meantime, a balance must be struck, and this remains the challenge for the church today. The church goes about the task of "seasoning" the surrounding culture (1989:220) and in this way creates the climate that will allow the realization of the program sanctioned by the vision of Galatians 3:28. But the church's "enactment" of that principle depends upon society's readiness (1989:221). With respect to women, then, the paraenesis of the Pastorals does not contradict the Pauline principle. Rather—and Towner argues this is the "only universal aspect of the teaching"—believers ought to participate in the institutions of society, keeping a finger on the pulse for the sake of the advancement of the gospel (1989:221).

The Pastoral Epistles and Women

Philip Towner's book was published as recently as 1989. Modern Western society has long subscribed to the principle of equality enshrined in Galatians 3:28, even if there is much work to be done. Many of the churches are unwilling, in Towner's terms, to be "seasoned," while "host" societies enact legislation ensuring the removal of gender and racial discrimination, equality of the sexes, and equal opportunity of employment. Paradoxically, then, it is these churches—the supposed guardians of the moral vision encapsulated in Galatians 3:28—that are not ready to remove barriers raised by passages such as 1 Timothy 2:9–15 and to allow women to enjoy equal access to and responsible participation in the leadership of the church.

In her commentary on the Pastorals (1996a) Margaret Davies concludes her discussion of the contentious passage 1 Timothy 2:9–15 and its appeal to the primacy of the male in the creation narrative of Genesis 2 with the remark that the reasons given for excluding women from exercising teaching roles within the church are unconvincing (cf. 1996b:86–87). They scarcely "bear scrutiny," she writes (1996a:19). The Pastor mounts the argument as a reaction to what she terms a countercultural "new Christian ethos" articulated in Galatians 3:28 and which Paul supports and encourages in Romans 16, 1 Corinthians 7 and 11, and Philippians 4:2–3. As a result, 1 Timothy has not accorded women the "responsible agency" it accords believing men, and limits what it asserts elsewhere of the effects of God's mercy and grace (1996a:20). Churches have thus been deprived of women's valuable service in public teaching and in other public roles.

While it is easy to be aware of the unacceptability of these injunctions, Davies reminds her readers that it is often difficult for us to acknowledge our own cultural presuppositions. Sexism, racism, and classism, she argues, are still present in our society. Against these, 1 Timothy presents a Christ who is mediator between God and all humankind, urges believers to pray for all, and contends that grace can transform us. Jouette Bassler's analysis of 1 Timothy 2:8–3:1a reveals a similar perception of the contemporary unacceptability of the Pastor's injunctions regarding the role of women in the church (1996:63). While the author is an inventive exegete of biblical narrative—Bassler has the Pastor's use of the creation account of Genesis 2 in mind—the conclusions drawn pose "the gravest hermeneutical challenge" (1996:63).

This conclusion receives no assent from the editors of and contributors to an anthology of essays entitled *Women in the Church: A Fresh Analysis of 1 Timothy 2:9–15*. In the Epilogue (1995:209–11), writing on behalf of all the contributors, the editors take their stand on the sole authority of the Bible. The enterprise represented by their book has been prompted by the belief that in the past "a certain view of women" may have been defended because of cultural prejudice (1995:209). Therefore all the contributors have analyzed the biblical evidence in order to see if 1 Timothy 2:9–15 justifies the continued maintenance of "role distinctions" in the church. They resoundingly answer yes. Paul's arguments are based on "universal norms" (1995:210). He applied these to the specific situation in Ephesus. His restrictions on the ministry of women were not culturally conditioned. Rather, his teaching is rooted in the created order. In the modern context, no woman should proclaim the Word of God from the pulpit "to the congregation of the saints." There are gray areas for further discussion, such as the teaching activity of women in the mission field, in Sunday school (where some male students might be approaching manhood), or at a seminary. What is clear, though, is that the church should not take its cue from the surrounding world and succumb to its pressure. Accordingly, the editors adopt a defiant stance in the face of Towner's hope that a "seasoned" society might encourage the church to "enact" the program outlined in Galatians 3:28 that the Pastor puts on hold until society is ready.

Raymond E. Brown

Raymond Brown's "The Pauline Heritage in the Pastorals: The Importance of Church Structure" (1984:31–46) underscores the contribution of the letters to our understanding of the development of church structures in the post-apostolic era. The presbyter-bishops are envisaged as official teachers. They reject any novel teaching, and protect and inculcate the deposit of faith. That they are to be recruited from the ranks of suitably qualified male householders underscores the community-protecting and stabilizing function Brown sees them providing. The Pastor, he argues, is endeavoring to structure a community in the face of forces that have the potential to cause the disintegration of the church. The charismatic endowments that made the historical Paul such a dynamic itinerant missionary are sacrificed to the more "pedestrian" qualities that will promote stability and harmony in the church. Are the letters' qualifications for leadership eternally valid? No, Brown replies. They have to do with public respectability in the context of a particular culture and "can and should" change over time (1984:36). Neither should we lament the letters' witness to the process of institutionalization, as have many scholars (chiefly Lutheran) who see the Pastorals as documents of "early Catholicism." If the church is a society, Brown contends, regulations are an "inevitable sociological development" (1984:37).

Brown isolates three strengths and weaknesses in the letters' stress on church structure. The first of these relates to the role of the leadership as the designated protectors of the apostolic deposit. Here Brown detects the "ancestor" of the various forms of ecclesiastical control by which orthodoxy protects itself from innovation. Yet the strategy developed by the Pastor in the struggle with proto-Gnostics is precisely that utilized by Irenaeus (ca. 180) in his *Adversus haereses* (ANF 1.315–567), his counter to the Gnostics. He too insists on a "pedigreed tradition," invoking links between the apostolic era and approved contemporary church officials. In times of doctrinal crisis, Brown argues, having a firm grasp of the trustworthy word (Titus 1:9) is an essential weapon. Control is necessary in the face of anarchy. However, the weakness of this approach is that official teaching becomes a way of life. Read without context, the Pastorals seem to sanction "a universal and unconditioned policy" to be brought to bear on all innovative thinking (1984:39). There are times when relaxation of control is warranted. Being inquisitive is necessary, Brown urges, lest the spirit of Jesus be suppressed. At times having no ideas is a greater peril than the danger posed by new ideas. Each generation, Brown contends, "must add to the deposit through its unique experience of Christ in its time" (1984:40).

The second relates to the Pastorals' conception of church order and the question of its continued validity. There are times when the church needs the innovator or the brilliant but disturbing leader. However, the church has often invoked what Brown calls the "Caiaphas principle" (see John 11:50) to deal with such people (1984:42). Dynamic mission may not be served well by "highly prudential leaders" committed to holding on to the past.

Third, Brown draws attention to the division in the letters between those who teach and those who are taught. The Pastorals vituperate other teachers who do not belong to the official circle. Unfortunately, Brown observes, the letters present a dualistic picture of true and counterfeit teachers. Church life, however, is "scarcely dualistic" (1984:43). Sometimes constructive teachers question the deposit of faith. Galileo is an example of such a teacher. 2 Timothy 3:6–7 singles out women who are dismissed as "weak-willed" and who are an easy prey to the false teachers. Even if it does not include all women, the injunction is demeaning (1984:94). The exclusion of all women from public teaching in 1 Timothy 2:12 is the practical result. Brown contends that some lay people, once instructed in the faith, are quite capable of teaching even the presbyter-bishops. It is wrong to shield believers from passages such as 2 Timothy 3:1–9. Unless they hear, intelligent lay people will never have the opportunity to ask "constructive questions that will lead them to recognize the human conditioning in the biblical content" (1984:44).[1] Finally, in the conclusion of his book (1984:146–50), Brown reminds his readers that the post-apostolic deposit, the Pastorals included, witnesses to the diversity of the New Testament. Some resist this on the basis of a doctrine of inspiration which teaches that if God is the author of scripture, then what God inspires must be harmonious and uniform. The propositions of scripture, understood literally, must be consistent and eternally valid. Others resist on the basis that, if Jesus planned the church, the apostles simply worked out in practice what Jesus had taught and directed them to do.

Jürgen Roloff

Roloff concludes his commentary on 1 Timothy with an overview that addresses the significance of the Pastoral Epistles as a corpus (1988:376–90). The letters, Roloff argues, seek to address believers in Pauline churches in a way that furthers the authority of the apostle and intelligibly interprets his message. Yet, while the letters focus exclusively on Paul as the sole apostle and guarantor of the faith, the Pastor articulates a diverse, almost "catholic," set of theological traditions in the name of Paul in order to consolidate and promote the church's existence in the world (1988:382).

The Pastoral Epistles, Roloff observes, take up positions with respect to the church's relationship to society that are diametrically opposed to those enunciated in Revelation, which circulated at the same time as the Pastorals in the Pauline communities of Asia Minor. This helps to explain the stress on God's universal saving intentions in the letters (1 Tim 2:4–6; Titus 2:11), the universal educative effect of the "appearance" of Christ (Titus 2:11–14), the positive view of creation (1 Tim 4:3–4), and the confidence that the Christian life resonates with the ethical ideals of society (1988:383). Furthermore, Roloff argues that the Pastorals have been influential in providing a filter through which to interpret the historical Paul. Seen in this way, Paul's intense eschatological expectation and his ethical rigor are softened and blurred, resulting in a Paul with whom the church has been able to live more easily over the centuries (1988:386). Roloff notes that the letters have provoked divergent responses from scholars in the traditions of Catholic and Protestant *(Evangelische)* theology. Scholars in the latter tradition have sharpened the contrast between the Paul of the undisputed letters and the Paul of the Pastorals. Scholars in the Catholic tradition have celebrated the fact that the Pastor has brought the angular, difficult Paul into the mainstream. Roloff suggests that these two approaches taken individually do not do sufficient justice to the Pastorals. Protestant scholarship should be able to appreciate the insight that the Pastor performed a great service to the church at a time of transition and crisis. The Pastorals seek to answer questions concerning the identity of the church, its organization, and its relationship to the wider society. In many ways, Roloff observes, the situation of the church today is analogous. On the other hand, the pluralism of present Western society and the erosion of ethical norms seems to have rendered utopian any hope that Christian life might fully express the ideals of the host culture (1988:389). For that reason, it may well be that we feel we have more in common with the social alienation encapsulated in Revelation than with the moral vision of the Pastorals and their sense of the compatibility of the ethics of church and society. Accordingly, he contends that modern interpreters of the New Testament gospel, having reflected on the options for relating to society modeled by the Pastorals and Revelation, need to chart a course that enables the church to continue to engage society without betraying the integrity of its message. The confidence that the gospel addresses perpetually contemporary concerns is the significant and distinctive contribution of the Pastorals to this urgent challenge.

J. Christiaan Beker

Beker's approach to the contemporary significance of the Pastoral Epistles is an integral part of his discussion of the post-Pauline deposit of the New Testament in his *Heirs of Paul* (1991:36–47, 83–86, 105–8). The post-Paulines are the first attempts to adapt the Pauline message in the acknowledgment that the particularities of Paul's day no longer apply. The new situations of the Pauline churches demanded re-interpretations of the Pauline gospel and not what Beker calls "a literal transposition" (1991:43) of Paul's message as though later contexts were either somehow identical or unimportant.

That the Pastor was eager to address the contingencies of his communities is undoubted. However, he does so not by engaging the false teachers, but by mandating a fixed theological construct authorized by the apostle who is now presented as a dogmatic, authoritarian figure. This construct is to be passed on as a "deposit" to succeeding generations. In his polemic, "Paul" seeks to drown his opponents in a "sea of rhetorical attacks," vilifying and stereotyping them (1991:46). The Pastor constructs a universally applicable apostle in which the continuity of the tradition is preserved at the expense of the particularities of history (1991:106). Beker laments the fact that the letters have lost Paul's distinctively dialog ical way of doing theology. Furthermore, his apocalyptic understanding of the Christ event, which is mediated to his addressees by means of symbols and metaphors (such as redemption, freedom, justification, being in Christ), is not expressed. Instead we encounter a cautious accommodation to the values of the host culture, the commendation of the ideal of a quiet life, and a concern for church order and administration. These overshadow the Pastor's commitment to the eschatological denouement (1991:44).

But the Pastorals are not to be dismissed. They and the other post-Paulines can help us frame contemporary solutions to the particularity of Paul's letters. At least the Pastorals show us that Paul cannot be literally reproduced (1991:106). Also inadequate is the approach that permits and even necessitates a multiplicity of interpretations, as many as there are interactions with the text, as this fails to safeguard the "normativity" of the biblical text (1991:120). He is also critical of Elisabeth Schüssler Fiorenza for urging a paradigm of biblical revelation in which the Bible is a "prototype," open to transformation and ongoing history, rather than a timeless and frozen "archetype" legitimating repressive ideals.[2] Instead, Beker advocates interpreting Paul in a way that faithfully transmits his message through the imaginative use of his symbols and metaphors while intelligibly engaging the present (1991:123–24).

Frances Young

Frances Young has articulated her sense of the contemporary significance of the Pastoral Epistles in an article (1992:105–20) and in the concluding chapter of her noteworthy contribution to the Cambridge New Testament Theology series (1994a). In the former she addresses how best to read the letters in the light of the distance between the implied readers (the original hearers of the letters) and actual readers today. Young advocates what she terms an "ethical reading" in which, on the one hand, the actual reader is respectfully open to what is being communicated while, on the other, free to retain a critical distance from the text as a modern person (1992:110). This sets up a dialectical relationship between the responses of the implied readers and actual readers today. There can be no doubting, Young confesses, the differences between the world of the text and the modern world. The implied readers espouse beliefs and an allegiance to cultural conventions that in many cases we only partially share or do not share at all. Some texts, such as 1 Timothy 2:11–15, are "hard, if not impossible" for today's readers (1992:113).

Young is fully cognizant of the rhetorical dynamic at work in the letters. She notes that persuasion to any writer or speaker's point of view requires the audience's assent to the subject matter and the arguments employed *(logos)* and the demonstration that the speaker/writer is trustworthy *(ethos),* and requires that it be moved to respond affirmatively to the speaker's point of view *(pathos).* The fact that the letters are pseudonymous raises the unavoidable question of whether it is possible to welcome them "with courtesy" and without suspicion (1992:106). However, readers today may still enter into the world of the text, and be persuaded, engaged, and moved to action. Yet readers also reserve their right, as responsible modern people, to exercise their discrimination, to withhold assent and maintain their critical distance. Responsible readers should be attentive to the past meaning and future potential of these texts. They should determine, Young concludes, not only the extent to which the actual author's claim to be passing on authoritative Pauline tradition is a valid one but also the ways the tradition might be developed further and rethought (1992:120). Readers should consider the potential of these texts to challenge and inspire churches to real reform. Perhaps, in this way, we might move beyond the suspicion and neglect with which the letters have been accorded.

Young builds on these conclusions in the concluding chapter of her *Theology* (1994a:145–61). She observes that Paul has been mediated to the church through the Pastorals. The letters have exerted a powerful influence by legitimating a pattern of hierarchical relationships within society, the church, and the family. Women have been subordinated and devalued, a state of affairs for which the letters bear considerable responsibility. In fact, they sanction what Young calls a "top-down culture of subordination" (1994a:147). A repressive social order has been "projected into the heavens" and portrayed as the divine will beyond the cultural specificity in which the Pastorals were crafted. One could simply regard this order as obsolete and out of date. However, Young wants to discover and to affirm the "spirit" of the letters and the tradition they bring to speech.

Adopting an incarnational model, Young proceeds to argue that the letters embody "two natures"—the divine and the human—in which historical particularity mediates the eternal (1994a:150). In the Pastorals one meets the sacred in the particular. Just as the Pastor sought to meet the challenges of the particular moment, so, Young contends, the letters teach us to embody our loyalty to Christ within our own cultural context in the midst of everyday life, affirming the good things of the created and the social order, and not in ascetic abandonment or Gnostic speculation. Noting the Pastor's strong affirmation of the social order, Young urges believers likewise to embrace the order around us since, as the Pastor observed, it has its source in God (1994a:153).[3] The letters teach us to live responsibly, yet exercising critical discernment and judgment with respect to present-day cultural mores and habits. Seeds of the critique of hierarchically ordered relationships so prominent in the codes of the Pastorals, though by no means absent from our own cultures, lie in the letters' teaching of the submission of all, leaders included, to the way of the servant (1994a:159). As for leaders, Young observes that the letters have more to do with the inculcation of Christian character than with function. Thus the letters offer a critique of the "way of power." Herein lies the stimulus for believers' to leaven present social structures by responsible participation in them, just as the early Christians did not leave the Greco-Roman household unchanged. Ultimately, Young concludes, the challenge arising out of the Pastorals for believers today is to embody Christian character in a pluralistic environment and to safeguard tradition in a manner that faithfully articulates its spirit.

Conclusion

Accorded the status of scripture in the early church, the Pastoral Epistles can rightly claim to be authoritative for establishing faith and doctrine. Yet they sanction a view of family life and mandate hierarchical social ideals that many interpreters of scripture, themselves informed by God's revelation, find confrontational and alien. However, for some scholars the letters present modern readers with universally true, normative prescriptions for Christian families and congregations. The program of the letters

should be adhered to or implemented even if that agenda is countercultural. The hermeneutical challenges they present are just as
keenly felt by those scholars who do not doubt their authenticity
and integrity as documents written by Paul but who reject the
claim of the literal, universal applicability of all the propositions
contained in them.

As we have seen in this chapter, the majority of scholars
surveyed contend that all scripture, the Pastorals included,
must be creatively and imaginatively engaged and interpreted
if its message and its claim is to be heard by our contemporaries. Only in that way will the authority of scripture be
authentically and intelligibly affirmed in the church today. A
number of scholars express their impatience with debates about
authorship and the question of the validity of the Pastor's actualization of the Pauline message. This writer's view is that
these matters will continue to be significant issues if only
because they confront the reader with fundamental questions
regarding the nature of scripture itself. Raymond Brown is correct, I believe, to insist that we hear all the text of the letters
(1984:44). Only in this way will the intelligent believer come
to appreciate the historical conditionality and acculturation of
that word. This, as Brown rightly points out, is an essential
aspect of understanding the incarnation itself. Moreover, the
letters challenge us to insightful and imaginative interpretation.
Those who are not committed to a literalist hermeneutic must
discover in what ways believers today might authentically
appropriate the spirit of the message of the letters.

Finally, Jürgen Roloff has observed that there no longer
continues to be a considerable degree of consonance and compatibility between society's structures and ethical ideals and
those affirmed and mandated by the Pastor. Since modern
Western societies are increasingly pluralistic and ethically rela-
tivistic, it will become increasingly difficult to follow consis-
tently the advice of scholars who argue that the Pastoral
Epistles challenge us to live an *inculturated* embodiment of the

Christian life, respecting society's structures and ethical ideals. Nevertheless, the Pastorals provide a fruitful model for determining how best the legacy of the past might serve the contemporary mission and message of the church. In a pluralistic world, the necessity to authentically engage society with the claims of the Christian message and to take up boldly the opportunity to incarnate the character of the Christian life of service in the name of God and his Christ remains the urgent task of all guardians of the apostolic deposit.

Notes

1. The Authorship of the Pastoral Epistles

1. See A Committee of the Oxford Society of Historical Theology 1905:95–96 for 1 Timothy 6:7, 10 in Polycarp, *Letter to the Philippians* 4.1, and 1905:97 for 2 Timothy 4:10 in Polycarp, *Letter to the Philippians* 9.2. However, Dibelius-Conzelmann 1972:85–86 argue that both writers are invoking widely attested gnomic sayings. See also Barnett 1941:182–83.

2. *Against Marcion* 5.21 (ANF 3.473–74). The fourth-century writer Epiphanius also asserts that Marcion rejected the Pastorals. Apparently, later Marcionites did include the Pastorals in their canons (see Blackburn 1948:52–53).

3. Kenyon 1936:xii. Quinn 1974:379–85 conjectures that (P46 was intended to be a codex of letters to churches. On the other hand, (P32 (ca. 200 C.E.), which comprises Titus 1:11–15 and 2:3–8, was originally a corpus of Paul's letters to individuals (cf. Kenyon 1936:xi). In a recent article Jeremy Duff 1998:578–90 disputes the claim of Kenyon and other scholars that there was insufficient space for the Pastorals in the codex. For this reason, he concludes, P46 in its extant form cannot be used to argue the case that the letters did not belong to the accepted Pauline corpus in Egypt ca. 200.

4. Harrison's enterprise is critiqued by Metzger in his survey of English, German, and Swedish scholarship on the issue in 1958:91–94. Metzger asks (1) whether the Pastorals and the rest of the Paulines are long enough to warrant conclusions about an author's style, (2) how

different the results of comparison can be before they throw doubt on a theory of common authorship, (3) how much allowance should be made for differences in subject matter and literary form between two texts, and (4) whether it is correct to argue that two works are necessarily more similar if they are by the same author than if they are not.

5. The Muratorian Canon testifies to Paul's mission to Spain. For other material connecting Paul with a Spanish mission, see *Acts of Peter* (*Actus Vercellenses* 1–3) (ca. 180–90). For text, see W. Schneemelcher (ed.), *The New Testament Apocrypha* (Louisville: Westminster/John Knox, 1992), 2.285–321 (287–89).

6. For a recent discussion of the use of secretaries in the ancient world and the Pauline letters, see Richards 1991. Despite the fact that no secretary is mentioned in the Pastoral Epistles either in prescript or postscript, as is the case of the use of secretaries in the Pauline corpus (see Rom 16:22; 1 Cor 16:21; Gal 6:11), Richards seems reluctant to rule out the influence of one. Furthermore, he does not consider the possibility that the letters were written neither by Paul nor his secretary.

7. See also Quinn 1978:62–75. Quinn explores the possibility that the Pastorals comprise the third volume projected by Luke, with Luke and Acts constituting the first two volumes.

8. See the subsequent response of Harrison 1964:17. Harrison contends that 95 of the hapaxes of the Pastorals do not occur in the Septuagint.

9. See also the discussion of the style and vocabulary of the Pastorals in Guthrie 1990:224–40. He invokes the following reasons for not attributing the letters to a pseudepigrapher: (1) dissimilarity of subject matter between them and the rest of the Pauline corpus, and the presence of new themes, (2) variations due to advancing age, (3) enlargement of vocabulary in a changed environment, and (4) a difference in recipients (since the Pastorals are private, not public, letters like the rest of the Pauline corpus).

10. Readers should weigh Spicq's comments on the "new day" for the church in 1969:1.294–5. For a contrasting view, see Beker 1980:331–37. Citing Romans 15:25–26, Beker argues that the collection is central both in demonstrating the priority of Jewish Christianity and the essential unity of Jew and Greek in the church. Furthermore, Romans 9–11 is an eloquent testimony to Paul's conviction that his Gentile mission has the conversion of Israel as its proper focus (cf. Käsemann 1969:241).

11. Towner (1994:17–19) contends that the mission to Crete (see Titus 1:5) could have been undertaken from Ephesus in the interval between Acts 19:20 and 21.

12. For further discussions of the view that pseudepigrapha are exercises in unethical deception, see the influential contributions of Candlish 1891:91–107, 262–79 and Torm 1977:111–48.

13. See the succinct rejoinder by Wall 1995:125–28. The belief that the Pastorals were written by Paul, he contends, is a "theological judgment about their continuing authority within the faith community" (1995:126–27) and their acceptance as vehicles of Pauline tradition.

14. See *Republic* 2.376E–383C; 389B; 414C–E. See also *Laws* 5.730C. The "noble lie" pervades Christian tradition. See also Donelson 1986:18–23. He cites, for example, Origen, *Against Celsus* 4.19, noting that Origen actually cites *Republic* 2.389B as justification.

15. Donelson 1986:21–22 is one of a number of scholars who discuss the presbyter Salvian (first half of the fifth century), who produced a treatise on wealth entitled *Timothei ad ecclesiam*. Called to account, the presbyter mounts the only known defense of the practice of writing pseudepigrapha emanating from the ancient world. Salvian refers to the writer of the treatise indirectly, thus maintaining his mask. The pseudepigrapher, he argues, needed to gain a hearing for an important message regarding materialism, something that would not have happened if the author had used his own name. Besides, Salvian concludes, the value of any book lies not in its authorship but in its intrinsic worth. For the text of Salvian's defense, see O'Sullivan 1947:256–63. For a sympathetic assessment, see Haefner 1934:8–15. On the other hand, the Wisdom of Solomon, which contains an explicit claim of Solomonic authorship, was universally regarded as scripture even by authorities who rejected the claim. The Muratorian Canon actually lists Wisdom (including it in the New Testament canon) in the knowledge that it was not written by Solomon but by "friends in his honor." The first father to express doubts about the almost universal attribution of the book to Solomon (see Wis 7:1–22a; 8:17–18) was Augustine. Yet he retained the book in his canon.

16. Tertullian's comment in his *Against Marcion* 4.5 (ANF 3.350) concerning the authorship of the Gospels of Mark and Luke are apposite. "[T]hat [Gospel] which Mark published," he writes, "may be affirmed to be Peter's whose interpreter Mark was. For even Luke's form of the Gospel men usually ascribe to Paul. And it may well seem that the works

which disciples publish belong to their masters." See also the surveys of pseudepigrapha in Mark Kiley 1986:15–35 and Richard J. Bauckham 1988:469–94.

17. Ca. 200 Tertullian wrote a treatise on baptism. In ch. 17 he speaks against the presumption of lay people to administer this sacrament without episcopal approval and in nonexceptional cases. He is also aware that a certain woman, who also presumes to teach, is appealing to the *Acts of Paul*, in which a woman (Thecla) baptizes herself and is set aside to preach by Paul, no less, as justification for the extension to women of the right to teach and baptize. He remarks that a certain Asian presbyter was removed from office because he had lately written the work "out of love for Paul" (*On Baptism*, 17 [ANF 3.677]). It was important, therefore, that the spurious nature of the *Acts* be discovered lest it give license for women to teach and to baptize. The *Acts of Paul* is scarcely credible, Tertullian writes, because the apostle, who did not even permit a woman "to learn with overboldness," would scarcely give women authority to teach and baptize. In Eusebius, *Ecclesiastical History* 6.12.6, Serapion, Bishop of Antioch, finally condemned the *Gospel of Peter*, a document used by the community at Rhossus, because he discovered docetic teaching in it. At first he was prepared to tolerate its use, although he did not know this gospel among the writings of Peter "handed down to us." For a recent account of the process of canonization in the early church, see Lee M. McDonald 1995. McDonald argues that, of his five criteria of canonicity (usage, apostolicity, antiquity, inspiration, and orthodoxy) usage is the most significant (1995:246–49). "It appears," he concludes, "the writings that were believed to have best conveyed the earliest Christian proclamation and that also best met the growing needs of the local churches in the third and fourth centuries were the writings they [the fathers] selected for their sacred scriptures" (1995:248).

18. However, see the judicious comments of Metzger 1972:22 n.67 and Donelson 1986:201. Donelson is worth citing: "The embarrassment of pseudepigraphy strikes at the heart of scriptural authority. The vehemence of conservative scholars who resist the whole notion of pseudepigraphy in the canon is well-founded, for to admit it would be to admit that the canon is not what they want it to be."

2. The Pastoral Epistles and Pauline Tradition

1. See Barnett 1941:251–77. See also Harrison 1921:167–75; Roloff 1988:39–40. For evidence that a collection of Paul's letters was in existence in the early second century, see 2 Peter 3:15–16 and Ignatius, *Letter to the Ephesians* 12.2.

2. See Conzelmann 1965–66:231–44; Schenke 1975:505–18; Meade 1986:9–10.

3. Deuteronomy 25:4 is cited in 1 Corinthians 9:9 and 1 Timothy 5:18 (cf. 2 Tim 2:6). Deuteronomy 19:15 is cited in 2 Corinthians 13:1 and 1 Timothy 5:19.

4. On this issue, see Marshall 1996:339–58. Marshall argues that the Pauline teaching on faith and "works of the law" in the undisputed letters is interpreted by post-Pauline interpreters in Ephesians and the Pastorals as meaning that Paul denied "that God acted in Christ on the basis of human works that might have predisposed him to favour humankind" (1996:358). Marshall thus questions the view that equates the Pauline "works of the law" with the "badges" of a Jewish profession.

5. The paraenesis of, say, Titus 2:9–10, 12 is grounded in the proclamation *(kerygma)* articulated in 2:11. See also the connection between the paraenesis of Titus 3:8 and the kerygmatic formulation of 3:4–7.

6. See Lohfink 1981:92. See also his list of early fathers in support of this suggestion at n.57. See, for example, Tertullian, *Scorpiace* 15 (ANF 3.648) and *Against all Heresies* 1 (ANF 3.650).

7. Lohfink observes that the Pastor is quite able to distinguish "deposit" from "teaching," as he does in 2 Timothy 1:14 ("my deposit") and 3:10 ("my teaching").

8. Wolter 1988:125 distinguishes "deposit" (Gr.: *paratheke*) and "tradition" (Gr.: *paradosis*) as follows. A founder of a school or movement (an Epicurus or a Paul) can bequeath a "deposit" to his followers. They, in turn, can "pass it on" (Gr.: *paradidomai*) (see Diogenes Laertius, *Lives of the Philosophers* 10.17).

9. Pagels 1975:166 nn.41, 42 is aware of only one instance. Clement, *Stromateis* 4.9 (ANF 2.422) cites Heracleon, who may be alluding to 2 Timothy 2:13. Incidentally, Pagels errs in giving Clement, *Stromateis* 2.13 and 1 Timothy 2:13 as references.

10. There have been several recent discussions of the implications of the book for the study of the New Testament and the early church. See, for example, Harrington 1980:289–98 (1982:162–73); N. Young 1994:178–97.

11. See Elisabeth Schüssler Fiorenza's survey of the role of early Christian women in positions of leadership in 1979:29–70.

12. In addition to *On Baptism* 17, see also *Prescription against Heretics* 41 (ANF 3.263) and *On the Veiling of Virgins* 9 (ANF 4.33).

13. As we have seen above, according to Tertullian, a lately defrocked (male) Asian presbyter wrote the *Acts of Paul*. Stevan Davies, who argues that the extant *Acts of Paul* was almost certainly written by a woman, suggests (unconvincingly) that Tertullian's report regarding the work is "not well informed" (1980:108).

14. See also Burrus 1987. Roman law required the marriage of virgins and the remarriage of widows. See Suetonius, *Augustus* 34 and Pomeroy 1995:161.

15. MacDonald proposes that the Pastorals are directly dependent on the *Acts of Paul* for some of the personalia of the letters. For example, Onesiphorus, Hermogenes, and Alexander the Coppersmith are mentioned only in the Pastorals and the *Acts*. See MacDonald's evidence in 1983:59–62. Positing the dependence on the part of the *Acts* fails to see that the direction of the polemic favors dependence on the part of the Pastorals.

16. Dunn 1993:258 also argues that the life of chastity was not chosen as a means of escape from male domination but because it was consistent with convictions of realized eschatology. However, these two alternatives are not as polar as Dunn suggests. Realized eschatology and a countercultural agenda are integrally linked, as in Brown 1988 (esp. chs. 1 and 2). Brown argues that early Christians believed that "[s]exual renunciation might lead the Christian to transform the body and, in transforming the body, to break with the discreet discipline of the ancient city" (1988:31). Nevertheless, as he points out (1988:156), late-second-century orthodox writers such as Tertullian and Clement of Alexandria did not envisage a renunciation of the institution of marriage on the part of the continent. They would have found the independent lifestyle of Thecla in the *Acts of Paul* unacceptable.

3. The Social Setting of the Pastoral Epistles

1. For further discussion, see Wilken 1971:268–91, Barton and Horsley 1981:7–26, and Kloppenborg 1996:16–30. For the relationship between the New Testament church and the associations, see Barton and Horsley 1981:27–41 and Meeks 1983:77–80 (who underscore the discontinuities) and McCready 1996:59–73 (who sees more evidence of continuity). Note also the survey in Ascough 1998:71–94.

2. See also L. Michael White's affirmations of Judge's insight into the relationship between the Greco-Roman social networks and the spread of Christianity in 1992:3–22 and 1992:23–36.

3. See, for example, Theissen 1982, Meeks 1983, Malherbe 1983, Stambaugh and Balch 1986, Kyrtatas 1987, and Osiek 1992. For an excellent introduction to the social context of the Pauline house churches, see Banks 1994.

4. See Plato, *Republic* 4.433A–434C; *Laws* 6.771E–7.824C; Aristotle, *Nicomachean Ethics* 8.x, and, most extensively, the majority of the first book of Aristotle's *Politics*. Aristotle's threefold pairing of a superior and an inferior, or ruler and subordinate, namely, husband/wife, father/child, and master/slave in the *Politics*, provides the best parallel to the New Testament codes.

5. See, for example, the comments on 1 Timothy 2:1–7 in Dibelius-Conzelmann 1972:40.

6. Balch and Osiek draw attention to the discussion in Schüssler Fiorenza 1983:169–75. She makes the point that in Romans 16:6, 12 Paul uses the same Greek verb, *kopian* (to work), of the women who "work" with him that he uses of his own enterprise of evangelizing and teaching (1983:169). Furthermore, in 1 Corinthians 16:16 Paul urges the addressees to be subject to every "co-worker and laborer" (cf. 1 Thess 5:12).

7. See Verner 1983:169–71. In common with the conventional wisdom of the day, the Pastor believes that men are fundamentally superior to women. This is demonstrated in two ways. First, the man was created before the woman (1 Tim 2:13). Second, 1 Timothy presents Eve's sin as a sexual transgression (2:14), reflecting a common early Jewish midrashic tradition (also found, incidentally, in 2 Cor 11:3). For this moral lapse a woman must win her salvation through childbearing, "a form of expiation commensurate with the crime attributed to her" (1983:170; cf. M. Y. MacDonald 1999:246). See also ch. 5, n. 5, below.

8. Slaves, Verner argues, were used to being called "brethren" in the church. But, he remarks, the "social attitudes which they faced directly contradicted the liberating, affirmative message they heard" (1983:185).

9. Verner 1983:186. On the role of women in the later New Testament, see, for example, Schüssler Fiorenza 1983:245–342 and M. Y. MacDonald 1999:236–53.

10. Towner draws the contrast unnecessarily tightly between himself and other scholars in the debate. There could be no successful urban mission on the part of the early church without an affirmation of Greco-Roman social values, precisely the matter urged by the Pastor. For the integral relationship between social networks and the spread of the new faith, see the articles by L. Michael White cited above (n.2).

11. For an influential treatment of the benefaction system see Danker 1982:esp. 317–493. Danker affirms Countryman's contention that the Pastor casts his appeal to the church leaders and the wealthy in terms redolent of the benefaction culture.

12. MacDonald adopts a stance critical of Judge in this respect. Whereas Judge is sceptical about employing models derived from environments other than those inhabited by the early Christians, she argues (with T. F. Carney) that "mind-sets dominate our thinking." She adds, "The concepts, arguments, assumptions and theories which are tied to the model-building process are constantly employed by everyone because they are the only conceptual tools available" (1988:26).

13. See Roloff 1988:169–78. Cf. Redalié 1994:350–51.

14. Young's views on the influence of the synagogue in the organization of the church in New Testament and subapostolic Christianity is mirrored in Burtchaell 1992:228–71, 272–338. Burtchaell believes that in era of the Acts, the Pastorals, and *1 Clement* the offices of elder and overseer are functionally identical (1992:296–97, 344–45). The roles first begin to be differentiated in Ignatius.

4. The Literary Setting of the Pastoral Epistles

1. Artemon's observation is cited in Demetrius, *On Style* 223 (text in Loeb Classical Library, trans. W. Rhys Roberts).

2. These two works are currently available in reprints published by Hendrickson.

3. See 1910:246. "Christianity in its earliest creative period was most closely bound up with the lower classes and had as yet no effective connection with the small upper class possessed of power and culture."

4. In his *Grunzüge griechisch-römischer Brieftopik* (1970), Klaus Thraede complements Koskenniemi's identification of the three characteristics of letters in the nonliterary papyri in his study of literary letters.

5. Malherbe notes Celsus's remark (preserved in Origen, *Contra Celsum* 1.4 [ANF 4.398]) that the Christians' system of ethics was borrowed from the philosophers.

6. The bulk of Malherbe's book comprises texts and translations of extant epistolary handbooks and ancient epistolary theorists.

7. The articles are "Paul: Hellenistic Philosopher or Christian Pastor" (Malherbe 1989:67–77), "'Gentle as a Nurse': The Cynic Background to 1 Thessalonians 2" (1989:35–48), "Medical Imagery in the Pastoral Epistles" (1989:121–36), and "'In Season and Out of Season': 2 Timothy 4:2" (1989:137–45). These were originally published in *Anglican Theological Review* 68 (1986), 3–13, *Novum Testamentum* 12 (1970), 203–17, in W. E. March (ed.), *Texts and Testaments: Critical Essays on the Bible and Early Christian Fathers* (San Antonio: Trinity University Press, 1980), 19–35, and *Journal of Biblical Literature* 103 (1984), 235–43, respectively.

8. For a fine survey of recent scholarship on the relationship between the Pauline churches and philosophical schools, see Ascough 1998:29–49.

9. This presentation, Martin argues, though intentional, is expressed implicitly rather than explicitly. Martin argues that (1) Paul is presented as a prophet, indeed, as the prophet like Moses, (2) like Moses, the successors Paul appoints as his legitimate heirs are also endowed with prophetic authority, (3) the role of Paul is analogous to that of a lawgiver whose successors are required to undertake all that Paul commands, and (4) like Moses, Paul is a suffering intercessor. The opponents of Paul are also presented in a manner that evokes the traditions about Moses' adversaries.

5. The Pastoral Epistles and Classical Rhetoric

1. See White 1983:435–36. See also Aune 1987:160 and Murphy-O'Connor 1995:65. For discussion of the "plain" style appropriate to a letter, as against the more florid and ornamented style required of the speech, see Demetrius, *On Style*, 223–35. Text in Malherbe 1988:16–19.

2. In this regard, two articles in the collection edited by Porter and Olbricht, *Rhetoric and the New Testament* (1993), are worth reading. They are Porter's "Rhetorical Categories in Pauline Literature" (100–22) and Jeffrey T. Reed's "Using Ancient Rhetorical Categories to Interpret Paul's Letters: A Question of Genre" (292–324).

3. See Judge 1968:37–50; Forbes 1986:1–30; Harding 1986:73–82.

4. *Art of Rhetoric*, I.iv.5. "Rhetoric is composed of analytical science and of that branch of political science which is concerned with ethics" (trans. Freese, LCL).

5. For this tradition see *4 Maccabees* 18:7–9 (mid-first century C.E.); *Apocalypse of Abraham* 23:1–5 (ca. 100 C.E.); *2 Enoch* 31:6 (ca. 100 C.E.); and the later Christian *Protevangelium of James* 13:1. Cf. 2 Corinthians 11:3. For the discussion of the background, see, for example, Hanson 1968:64–77 and related discussion in Stowers 1994:49–53, 93–95.

6. The Meaning of the Pastoral Epistles Today

1. Cf. Pontifical Biblical Commission 1993:113: "The Word of God finds expression in the work of human authors. The thought and the words belong at one and the same time both to God and to human beings, in such a way that the whole Bible comes at once from God and from the inspired human author. This does not mean, however, that God has given the historical conditioning of the message a value which is absolute" (cf. 1993:132–33). See also the apt concluding "epilogue" of Crouch's study of the Colossian *Haustafel* 1972:152–61. "The truth of the *Haustafel*," he writes, "which derives from its original situation and at the same time transcends the historically conditioned form of its exhortations lies in its demand that the man [*sic*] of faith affirm his own finitude and accept the 'givenness' of life within the social order" (1972:158).

2. Beker cites Schüssler Fiorenza 1983:33. Only those texts that break through patriarchal culture and "plausibility structures" are accorded the "theological authority of revelation" (1983:33). See also the comment in 1983:36: "Women as church have a continuous history and tradition that can claim Jesus and the praxis of the earliest church as its biblical root model or prototype, one that is open to feminist transformation."

3. Cf. Karris 1979:xvii: "Our salvation lies in the ordinariness of our fidelity to those commitments which make up our daily lives."

Select Bibliography

A Committee of the Oxford Society of Historical Theology. 1905. *The New Testament in the Apostolic Fathers*. Oxford: Clarendon.

Anderson, R. Dean, Jr. 1996. *Ancient Rhetorical Theory and Paul*. Kampen: Kok Pharos Publishing House.

Ascough, Richard S. 1998. *What Are They Saying About the Formation of Pauline Churches?* New York/Mahwah, N.J.: Paulist Press.

Aune, David E. 1987. *The New Testament in its Literary Environment*. Philadelphia: Westminster.

Balch, David L. 1981. *Let Wives be Submissive: The Domestic Code in 1 Peter*. SBLMS 26. Chico, Cal.: Scholars Press.

Balch, David L., and Carolyn Osiek. 1997. *Families in the New Testament World: Households and House Churches*. Louisville: John Knox.

Banks, Robert J. 1994. *Paul's Idea of Community*. Peabody: Hendrickson.

Barclay, John M. G. 1997. "The Family as the Bearer of Religion." In *Constructing Early Christian Families: Family as Social Reality and Metaphor*, ed. Halvor Moxnes, 66–80. London: Routledge.

Barnett, Albert E. 1941. *Paul Becomes a Literary Influence*. Chicago: Chicago University Press.

Barrett, C. K. 1970. *The Signs of an Apostle*. London: Epworth.

———. 1973–74. "Pauline Controversies in the Post-Pauline Period." *NTS* 20:229–45.

Barton, Stephen C., and Gregory H. R. Horsley. 1981. "A Hellenistic Cult Group and the New Testament Churches." JAC 24: 7–41.

Bassler, Jouette M. 1983. "The Widow's Tale: A Fresh Look at 1 Tim. 5:3–16." *JBL* 103:23–41.

———. 1996. *1 Timothy, 2 Timothy, Titus*. Nashville: Abingdon.

Bauckham, Richard J. 1988. "Pseudo-Apostolic Letters." *JBL* 107:469–94.

Bauer, Walter. 1971. *Orthodoxy and Heresy in Earliest Christianity*. Philadelphia: Fortress. Translation *Rechtgläubigkeit und Ketzerei im ältesten Christentum*. Tübingen: Mohr (Siebeck), 1934.

Beker, J. Christiaan. 1980. *Paul the Apostle: The Triumph of God in Life and Thought*. Philadelphia: Fortress.

———. 1991. *Heirs of Paul*. Philadelphia: Fortress.

Berger, Klaus. 1984. *Formgeschichte des Neuen Testaments*. Heidelberg: Quelle & Meyer.

Betz, Hans Dieter. 1979. *Galatians*. Philadelphia: Fortress.

Blackburn, Edwin C. 1948. *Marcion and His Influence*. London: SPCK.

Boughton, Lynne C. 1991. "From Pious Legend to Feminist Fantasy: Distinguishing Hagiographical License from Apostolic Practice in the *Acts of Paul/Acts of Thecla*." *JR* 71:362–83.

Brown, Peter R. L. 1988. *Body and Society: Men, Women, and Sexual Renunciation in Early Christianity*. New York: Columbia University Press.

Brown, Raymond E. 1984. *The Churches the Apostles Left Behind.* New York/Ramsey, N.J.: Paulist Press.

Brox, Norbert. 1969. *Die Pastoralbriefe.* Regensburg: Pustet.

———. 1975. *Falsche Verfasserangaben: Zur Erklärung der frühchristlichen Pseudepigraphie.* Stuttgart: KBW Verlag.

Burgess, T. C. 1902. "Epideictic Literature." *Chicago Studies in Classical Literature* 3:89–253.

Burrus, Virginia. 1987. *Chastity as Autonomy: Women in the Stories of Apocryphal Acts.* Lewiston/Ormiston, Maine: Edwin Mellen.

Burtchaell, James T. 1992. *From Synagogue to Church: Public services and offices in the earliest Christian communities.* Cambridge: Cambridge University Press.

Caird, George B. 1980. *The Language and Imagery of the Bible.* Philadelphia: Westminster.

Campbell, R. Alistair. 1994. *The Elders: Seniority within Earliest Christianity.* Edinburgh: T. & T. Clark.

von Campenhausen, Hans. 1963. "Polykarp von Smyrna und die Pastoralbriefe." In *Aus der Frühzeit des Christentums: Studien zur Kirchengeschichte des ersten und zweiten Jahrhunderts,* 197–252. Tübingen: Mohr (Siebeck).

Candlish, J. S. 1891. "On the Moral Character of Pseudonymous Books." *Exp* 4 series 4:91–107, 262–79.

Collins, John J. 1984. "Testaments." In *Jewish Writings of the Second Temple Period,* ed. Michael E. Stone, 325–55. Philadelphia/Assen: Fortress/Van Gorcum.

Collins, Raymond F. 1975. "The Image of Paul in the Pastorals." *LTP* 31:147–73.

Conzelmann, Hans. 1965–66. "Paulus und die Weisheit." *NTS* 12:231–44.

Countryman, L. William. 1980. *The Rich Christian in the Church of the Early Empire: Contradictions and Accommodations.* New York/Toronto: Edwin Mellen Press.

Crouch, James E. 1972. *The Origin and Intention of the Colossian Haustafel.* FRLANT 109. Göttingen: Vandenhoeck & Ruprecht.

Danker, Frederick W. 1982. *Benefactor: Epigraphic Study of a Graeco-Roman and New Testament Semantic Field.* St. Louis: Clayton Press.

Davies, Margaret. 1996a. *The Pastoral Epistles.* London: Epworth.

————. 1996b. *The Pastoral Epistles.* New Testament Guides. Sheffield: Academic Press.

Davies, Stevan L. 1980. *The Revolt of the Widows: The Social World of the Apocryphal Acts.* Carbondale and Edwardsville, Ill.: Southern Illinois University Press.

de Boer, Martinus C. 1980. "Images of Paul in the Post-Apostolic Period." *CBQ* 42:359–80.

Deissmann, G. Adolf. 1901. *Bible Studies: Contributions Chiefly from the Papyri and Inscriptions to the History of the Language, the Literature, and the Religion of Hellenistic Judaism and Primitive Christianity.* Edinburgh: T. & T. Clark.

————. 1910. *Light from the Ancient East: The New Testament Illustrated by Recently Discovered Texts of the Graeco-Roman World.* New York: George H. Doran.

Dibelius, Martin, and Hans Conzelmann. 1972. *The Pastoral Epistles.* Philadelphia: Fortress.

Donelson, Lewis R. 1986. *Pseudepigraphy and Ethical Argument in the Pastoral Epistles.* HUT 22. Tübingen: Mohr (Siebeck).

Doty, William. 1969. "The Classification of Epistolary Literature." *CBQ* 31:183–99.

————. 1973. *Letters in Primitive Christianity*. Philadelphia: Fortress.

Duff, Jeremy. 1998. "P46 and the Pastorals: A Misleading Consensus." *NTS* 44:578–90.

Dunn, Peter W. 1993. "Women's Liberation, the *Acts of Paul*, and other Apocryphal *Acts of the Apostles*." *Apocrypha* 4:245–61.

Easton, Burton Scott. 1947. *The Pastoral Epistles*. New York: Scribners.

Ellis, E. Earle. 1992. "Pseudonymity and Canonicity of New Testament Documents." In *Worship, Theology and Ministry in the Early Church: Essays in Honour of Ralph P. Martin*, eds. Michael J. Wilkins and Terence Paige, 212–24. JSNTSup 87. Sheffield: JSOT Press.

Fiore, Benjamin. 1986. *The Function of Personal Example in the Socratic and Pastoral Epistles*. AnBib 105. Rome. Biblical Institute.

Fitzgerald, John T. 1988. *Cracks in an Earthen Vessel: An Examination of the Catalogues of Hardships in the Corinthian Correspondence*. SBLDS 99. Atlanta: Scholars Press.

Forbes, Christopher. 1986. "Comparison, Self-Praise and Irony: Paul's Boasting and the Conventions of Hellenistic Rhetoric." *NTS* 36:1–30.

Funk, Robert W. 1967. "The Apostolic *Parousia*: Form and Significance." In *Christian History and Interpretation: Studies Presented to John Knox*, eds. W. R. Farmer, C. F. D. Moule, and R. R. Niebuhr, 249–68. Cambridge: Cambridge University Press.

Gealy, Fred D. 1955. "I and II Timothy, Titus." In *The Interpreter's Bible*, ed. George A. Buttrick, 11.353–551. 12 Volumes. Nashville: Abingdon.

Goodspeed, Edgar J. 1937. *New Chapters in New Testament Study*. New York: Macmillan.

Guthrie, Donald. 1990. *The Pastoral Epistles*. Leicester/Downers Grove, Ill.: IVP/Eerdmans.

Haefner, Alfred E. 1934. "A Unique Source for the Study of Ancient Pseudonymity." *ATR* 16:8–15.

Hahneman, Geoffrey M. 1992. *The Muratorian Fragment and the Development of the Canon*. Oxford: Clarendon.

Hanson, Anthony T. 1968. "Eve's Transgression." In *Studies in the Pastoral Epistles*, 64–77. London: SPCK.

———. 1968. "The Significance of the Pastoral Epistles." In *Studies in the Pastoral Epistles*, 110–20. London: SPCK.

———. 1981. "The Domestication of Paul: A Study in the Development of Early Christian Theology." *BJRL* 63:402–18.

———. 1982. *The Pastoral Epistles*. London: Marshall, Morgan & Scott.

Harding, Mark. 1986. "The Classical Rhetoric of Praise and the New Testament." *RTR* 45:73–82.

———. 1998. *Tradition and Rhetoric in the Pastoral Epistles*. StudBL 3. New York: Peter Lang.

Harrington, Daniel Y. 1980. "The Reception of Walter Bauer's *Orthodoxy and Heresy in Earliest Christianity* During the Last Decade." *HTR* 73:289–98. Reprinted in 1982, 162–73. *Light of All Nations: Essays on the Church in New Testament Research*. Wilmington, Del.: Michael Glazier.

Harrison, P. N. 1921. *The Problem of the Pastoral Epistles*. Oxford: Oxford University Press.

———. 1955. "Important Hypotheses Reconsidered III: The Authorship of the Pastoral Epistles." *ExpTim* 67:77–81.

———. 1964. *Paulines and Pastorals*. London: Villiers.

Hoffmann, R. Joseph. 1984. *Marcion: On the Restitution of Christianity*. Chico, Cal.: Scholars Press.

Holmberg, Bengt. 1980. *Paul and Power: The Structure of Authority in the Primitive Church as Reflected in the Pauline Epistles*. Philadelphia: Fortress.

Holtzmann, Heinrich J. 1880. *Die Pastoralbriefe kritisch und exegetisch untersucht*. Leipzig: Wilhelm Engelmann.

Howe, E. Margaret. 1980. "Interpretations of Paul in the *Acts of Paul/Thecla*." In *Pauline Studies: Essays presented to Professor F. F. Bruce on His 70th Birthday*, eds. Donald A. Hagner and Murray J. Harris, 33–49. Exeter: Eerdmans/Paternoster.

Johnson, Luke Timothy. 1978–79. "II Timothy and the Polemic Against False Teachers: A Re-examination." *JRelS* 6.2/7.1:1–26.

———. 1996. *Letters to Paul's Delegates: 1 Timothy, 2 Timothy, Titus*. Valley Forge, Penn.: Trinity Press International.

Judge, Edwin A. 1960a. *The Social Pattern of Christian Groups in the First Century: Some Prolegomena to the Study of New Testament Ideas of Social Obligation*. London: Tyndale.

———. 1960b. "The Early Christians as a Scholastic Community." *JRH* 1:4–15, 125–37.

———. 1968. "Paul's Boasting in Relation to Contemporary Professional Practice." *AusBR* 16:37–50.

———. 1972. "St. Paul and Classical Society." JAC 15:19–36.

Karris, Robert J. 1971. "The Function and Sitz im Leben of the Paraenetic Elements in the Pastoral Epistles." Th.D. Dissertation. Harvard University.

———. 1972. "The Polemic of the Pastoral Epistles." *JBL* 93:549–64.

———. 1979. *The Pastoral Epistles*. Wilmington, Del.: Michael Glazier.

Keck, Leander E. 1974. "On the Ethos of the Early Christians." *JAAR* 42:435–52.

Kennedy, George A. 1984. *New Testament Interpretation Through Rhetorical Criticism.* Chapel Hill, N.C.: University of North Carolina Press.

———. 1999. *Classical Rhetoric and its Christian and Secular Tradition from Ancient to Modern Times.* Second edition, revised and enlarged. Chapel Hill, N.C./London: University of North Carolina Press.

Kenny, Anthony J. P. 1986. *A Stylometric Study of the New Testament.* Oxford: Oxford University Press.

Kenyon, Frederic G. 1936. *The Chester Beatty Biblical Papyri: Descriptions and Texts of Twelve Manuscripts on Papyrus of the Greek Bible. Fasciculus III Supplement: Pauline Epistles.* London: Emery Walker.

Kidd, Reggie M. 1990. *Wealth and Beneficence in the Pastoral Epistles.* SBLDS 122. Atlanta: Scholars Press.

Kiley, Mark. 1986. *Colossians as Pseudepigraphy.* Sheffield: JSOT Press.

Kloppenborg, John S. 1996. "Collegia and *Thiasoi*: Issues in function, taxonomy and membership." In *Voluntary Associations in the Graeco-Roman World*, eds. John S. Kloppenborg and Stephen G. Wilson, 16–30. London/New York: Routledge.

Knight, George W. III. 1992. *The Pastoral Epistles.* Grand Rapids: Eerdmans.

Koester, Helmut. 1979. "I Thessalonians—Experiment in Christian Writing." In *Continuity and Discontinuity in Church History*, eds. F. F. Church and T. George, 33–44. Leiden: Brill.

Koskenniemi, Heikki. 1956. *Studien zur Idee und Phraseologie des griechischen Briefes bis 400 n. Chr.* Helsinki: Suomalainen Tiedeakatemia.

Köstenberger, Andreas J., Thomas R. Schreiner, and H. Scott Baldwin, eds. 1995. *Women in the Church: A Fresh Analysis of 1 Timothy 2:9–15.* Grand Rapids: Baker.

Kyrtatas, Dimitris J. 1987. *The Social Structure of the Early Christian Communities.* London/New York: Verso.

Lightfoot, J. B. 1885. *The Epistle to the Philippians.* London: Macmillan.

Lock, W. W. 1924. *A Critical and Exegetical Commentary on Pastoral Epistles.* Edinburgh: T. & T. Clark.

Lohfink, Gerhard. 1981. "Paulinische Theologie in der Rezeption der Pastoralbriefe." In *Paulus in den neutestamentlichen Spätschriften*, ed. Karl Kertelge, 50–121. Freiburg/Basel/Wien: Herder.

MacDonald, Dennis R. 1983. *The Legend and the Apostle: The Battle for Paul in Story and Canon.* Philadelphia: Westminster.

MacDonald, Margaret Y. 1988. *The Pauline Churches: A Socio-historical Study of Institutionalization in the Pauline and Deutero-Pauline Writings.* SNTSMS 60. Cambridge: Cambridge University Press.

———. 1996. *Early Christian Women and Pagan Opinion: The Power of the Hysterical Woman.* Cambridge: Cambridge University Press.

———. 1999. "Rereading Paul: Early Interpreters of Paul on Women and Gender." In *Women and Christian Origins*, eds. Ross Shepard Kraemer and Mary Rose D'Angelo, 236–53. New York: Oxford University Press.

Malherbe, Abraham J. 1983. *Social Aspects of Early Christianity.* Philadelphia: Fortress.

———. 1986a. *The Cynic Epistles.* SBL Resources for Biblical Study 12. Atlanta: Scholars Press.

———. 1986b. *Moral Exhortation: A Greco-Roman Sourcebook.* Philadelphia: Westminster.

———. 1987. *Paul and the Thessalonians: The Philosophic Tradition of Pastoral Care.* Philadelphia: Fortress.

———. 1988. *Ancient Epistolary Theorists.* SBL Resources for Biblical Study 19. Atlanta: Scholars Press.

———. 1989. *Paul and the Popular Philosophers.* Minneapolis: Fortress.

———. 1992. "Hellenistic Moralists and the New Testament." *ANRW* II 26.2:267–333.

Marshall, I. Howard. 1996. "Salvation, Grace and Works in the Later Writings in the Pauline Corpus." *NTS* 42:339–58.

Martin, Seán Charles. 1997. *Pauli Testamentum: 2 Timothy and the Last Words of Moses.* Rome: Gregorian University.

McCready, Wayne O. 1996. "EKKLĒSIA and Voluntary Associations." In *Voluntary Associations in the Graeco-Roman World,* eds. John S. Kloppenborg and Stephen G. Wilson, 59–73. London/New York: Routledge.

McDonald, Lee M. 1995. *The Formation of the Christian Biblical Canon.* Peabody, Mass.: Hendrickson.

McNamara, Jo Ann. 1983. *A New Song: Celibate Women in the First Three Centuries.* New York/Binghampton: Harrington Park Press.

Meade, David G. 1986. *Pseudonymity and Canon.* WUNT 39. Tübingen: Mohr (Siebeck).

Meeks, Wayne A. 1983. *The First Urban Christians: The Social World of the Apostle Paul.* New Haven/London: Yale University Press.

Metzger, Bruce M. 1958. "A Reconsideration of Certain Arguments Against the Pauline Authorship of the Pastoral Epistles." *ExpTim* 70:91–94.

————. 1972. "Literary Forgeries and Canonical Pseudepigrapha." *JBL* 91:3–24.

————. 1992. *The Text of the New Testament: Its Transmission, Corruption, and Restoration.* New York/London: Oxford University Press.

Miller, James D. 1997. *The Pastoral Letters as Composite Documents.* SNTSMS 93. Cambridge: Cambridge University Press.

Moule, C. F. D. 1965. "The Problem of the Pastoral Epistles." *BJRL* 47:430–52.

Murphy-O'Connor, Jerome. 1991. "2 Timothy Contrasted with 1 Timothy and Titus." *RB* 98:403–18.

————. 1995. *Paul the Letter-Writer: His World, His Options, His Skills.* Collegeville, Minn.: Liturgical Press.

Neumann, Kenneth J. 1990. *The Authenticity of the Pauline Epistles in the Light of Stylostatistical Analysis.* SBLDS 120. Atlanta: Scholars Press.

von Nordheim, Eckhard. 1980. *Die Lehre der Alten.* Two volumes. Leiden: Brill.

Oberlinner, Lorenz. 1994. *Kommentar zum ersten Timotheusbrief.* HTKNT XI.1. Freiburg: Herder.

————. 1995. *Kommentar zum zweiten Timotheusbrief.* HTKNT XI.2. Freiburg: Herder.

————. 1996. *Kommentar zum Titusbrief.* HTKNT XI.3. Freiburg: Herder.

Osiek, Carolyn. 1992. *What are They Saying about the Social Setting of the New Testament?* New York/Mahwah, N.J.: Paulist Press.

O'Sullivan, Jeremiah F. 1947. *The Writings of Salvian, the Presbyter.* In *Fathers of the Church*, volume 3. New York: Cima.

Pagels, Elaine. 1975. *The Gnostic Paul: Gnostic Exegesis in the Pauline Letters.* Philadelphia: Fortress.

Pomeroy, Sarah B. 1995. *Goddesses, Whores, Wives, and Slaves: Women in Classical Antiquity.* New York: Schocken.

Pontifical Biblical Commission. 1993. *The Interpretation of the Bible in the Church.* Boston: St. Paul Books and Media.

Porter, Stanley E. 1993. "Rhetorical Categories in Pauline Literature." In *Rhetoric and the New Testament*, eds. Stanley E. Porter and Thomas H. Olbricht, 100–122. Sheffield: JSOT Press.

———. 1995. "Pauline Authorship and the Pastoral Epistles: Implications for the Canon." *BBR* 5:105–23.

Prior, Michael. 1989. *Paul the Letter-Writer and the Second Letter to Timothy.* JSNTSup 23. Sheffield: JSOT Press.

Quinn, Jerome D. 1974. "P46—the Pauline Canon." *CBQ* 36:379–85,

———. 1978. "The Last Volume of Luke: The Relation of Luke-Acts and the Pastoral Epistles." In *Perspectives on Luke-Acts*, ed. Charles H. Talbert, 62–75. Macon, Ga.: Mercer.

———. 1981. "Paraenesis and the Pastoral Epistles." In *De la Tôrah au Messie*, eds. M. Carrez, J. Doré, and P. Grelot, 495–501. Paris: Desclée.

———. 1990. *The Letter to Titus.* New York: Doubleday.

Redalié, Yann. 1994. *Paul après Paul: Le temps, le salut, la morale selon les épîtres à Timothée et à Tite.* Geneva: Labor et Fides.

Reed, Jeffrey T. 1993. "Using Ancient Rhetorical Categories to Interpret Paul's Letters: A Question of Genre." In *Rhetoric and the New Testament*, eds. Stanley E. Porter and Thomas H. Olbricht, 292–324. Sheffield: JSOT Press.

Richards, E. Randolph. 1991. *The Secretary in the Letters of Paul.* WUNT 2.42. Tübingen: Mohr (Siebeck).

Roloff, Jürgen. 1988. *Der erste Brief an Timotheus.* EKKNT 15. Zürich: Benziger Verlag.

Ruether, Rosemary Radford. 1974. "Misogynism and Virginal Feminism in the Fathers of the Church." In *Religion and Sexism: Images of Woman in the Jewish and Christian Tradition*, ed. Rosemary Radford Ruether, 150–83. New York: Simon & Schuster.

Schenke, Hans-Martin. 1975. "Das Weiterwirken des Paulus und die Pflege seines Erbes durch die Paulus-Schule." *NTS* 21:505–18.

Schneemelcher, Wilhelm, ed. 1992. *New Testament Apocrypha. Volume Two: Writings Relating to the Apostles; Apocalypses and Related Subjects.* Revised Edition. Louisville: Westminster/John Knox.

Schulz, Siegfried. 1976. *Die Mitte der Schrift.* Berlin: Kreuz-Verlag.

Schüssler Fiorenza, Elisabeth. 1979. "Word, Spirit and Power: Women in Early Christian Communities." In *Women of Spirit*, eds. Rosemary Radford Ruether and Eleanor McLaughlin, 29–70. New York: Simon & Schuster.

———. 1983. *In Memory of Her: A Feminist Theological Reconstruction of Christian Origins.* New York: Crossroad.

Schwarz, Roland. 1983. *Bürgerliches Christentum im Neuen Testament?* Klosterneuberg: Verlag Österreichisches Katholisches Bibelwerk.

Spicq, Ceslaus. 1969. *Les Épîtres Pastorales.* Two volumes. Paris: Gabalda.

Stambaugh, John E., and David L. Balch. 1986. *The New Testament in Its Social Environment.* Philadelphia: Westminster.

Stirewalt, M. Luther Jr. 1993. *Studies in Ancient Greek Epistolography.* SBL Resources for Biblical Study 27. Atlanta: Scholars Press.

Stowers, Stanley K. 1984. "Social Status, Public Speaking and Private Teaching: The Circumstances of Paul's Preaching." *NovT* 26:59–82.

————. 1986. *Letter Writing in Greco-Roman Antiquity.* Philadelphia: Westminster.

————. 1994. *Rereading Romans: Justice, Jews, and Gentiles.* New Haven: Yale University Press.

Theissen, Gerd. 1982. *The Social Setting of Pauline Christianity: Essays on Corinth.* Philadelphia: Fortress.

Thraede, Klaus. 1970. *Grunzüge griechisch-römischer Brieftopik.* München: Beck.

————. 1977. "Ärger mit der Freiheit: Die Beziehung von Mann und Frau in Theorie und Praxis der alten Kirche." In *"Freunde in Christus werden.…"* Die Beziehung von Mann und Frau als Folge an Theologie und Kirche*, Gerta Scharffenorth and Klaus Thraede, 31–182. Gelnhausen/Berlin & Stein/Mfr: Burckhardthaus-Verlag & Laetare-Verlag.

Thurston, Bonnie B. 1989. *The Widows: A Women's Ministry in the Early Church.* Philadelphia: Fortress.

Torm, F. 1977. "Die Psychologie der Pseudonymität im Hinblick auf Literatur des Urchristentums." In *Pseudepigraphie in der heidnischen und jüdisch-christlichen Antike*, ed. Norbert Brox, 111–48. Darmstadt: Wissenschaftliche Buchgesellschaft.

Towner, Philip H. 1987. "Gnosis and Realized Eschatology in Ephesus." *JSNT* 31:95–124.

————. 1989. *The Goal of Our Instruction*. JSNTSup 34. Sheffield: JSOT Press.

————. 1994. *1–2 Timothy & Titus*. Downers Grove, Ill.: Intervarsity.

Trummer, Peter. 1978. *Die Paulustradition der Pastoralbriefe*. Frankfort am Main/Bern/Las Vegas: Lang.

————. 1981. "Corpus Paulinum—Corpus Pastorale." In *Paulus in den neutestamentlichen Spätschriften*, ed. Karl Kertelge, 122–46. Freiburg/Basel/Wien: Herder.

Verner, David C. 1983. *The Household of God: The Social World of the Pastoral Epistles*. SBLDS 71. Chico, Cal.: Scholars Press.

Vetschera, Rudolf. 1912. *Zur griechischen Paränese*. Smichow: Rohlicek & Sievers.

Wall, Robert W. 1995. "Pauline Authorship and the Pastoral Epistles: A Response to S. E. Porter." *BBR* 5:125–28.

Wegenast, Klaus. 1962. *Das Verständnis der Tradition bei Paulus und in den Deuteropaulinen*. Neukirchen: Neukirchener Verlag.

White, John L. 1983. "Saint Paul and the Apostolic Letter Tradition," *CBQ* 45:433–44.

————. 1984. "New Testament Epistolary Literature." *ANRW* II 25 2:1730–56.

————. 1986. *Light from Ancient Letters*. Philadelphia: Fortress.

White, L. Michael. 1992. "Finding the Ties that Bind: Issues from Social Description." *Semeia* 56:3–22.

————. 1992. "Social Networks: Theoretical Orientation and Historical Applications." *Semeia* 56:23–36.

Wilken, Robert L. 1971. "Collegia, Philosophical Schools, and Theology." In *The Catacombs and the Colosseum: The Roman Empire as the Setting of Primitive Christianity*, eds. Stephen Benko and John J. O'Rourke, 268–91. Valley Forge, Penn.: Judson Press.

Wilson, Stephen G. 1976. "The Portrait of Paul in Acts and the Pastorals." In *SBL Seminar Papers*, ed. George MacRae, 397–411. Missoula, Mont.: Scholars Press.

————. 1979. *Luke and the Pastoral Epistles*. London: SPCK.

Wolter, Michael. 1988. *Die Pastoralbriefe als Paulustradition*. Göttingen: Vandenhoeck and Ruprecht.

Young, Frances M. 1992. "The Pastoral Epistles and the Ethics of Reading." *JSNT* 45:105–20.

————. 1994a. *Theology of the Pastoral Epistles*. Cambridge: Cambridge University Press.

————. 1994b. "On ΕΠΙΣΚΟΠΟΣ and ΠΡΕΣΒΥΤΕΡΟΣ." *JTS* n.s. 45:142–48.

Young, Norman H. 1994. "The Sectarian Tradition in Early Christianity." *Prudentia Supplements*, 178–97.

Suggestions for Further Study

Balch, David L. 1981. *Let Wives be Submissive: The Domestic Code in 1 Peter.* SBLMS 26. Chico, Cal.: Scholars Press. An important resource with insightful discussion of the origins and function of the so-called household codes. The monograph concentrates in particular on the code in 1 Peter, and is essential reading for students wishing to understand the moral vision of the Pastorals.

Bassler, Jouette M. 1996. *1 Timothy, 2 Timothy, Titus.* Nashville: Abingdon. Bassler's commentary engages the reader with insightful comment on the text of the Pastoral Epistles in their late first century setting while addressing the urgent hermeneutical challenges of the letters.

Beker, J. Christiaan. 1991. *Heirs of Paul.* Philadelphia: Fortress. Beker applies his coherence/contingency model to the post-Pauline New Testament, the Pastoral Epistles included. He argues that the Pastor has failed to bring Paul's dialogical hermeneutic to speech, and has largely jettisoned his apocalyptic worldview in favor of accommodation with the prevailing moral expectations of Greco-Roman urban culture. Nevertheless, Beker argues that the Pastorals should provoke modern readers to take up the challenge of interpreting Paul's gospel intelligibly.

Brown, Raymond E. 1984. *The Churches the Apostles Left Behind.* New York/Ramsey, N.J.: Paulist Press. Written by one of the great New

Testament scholars of the twentieth century, the scope of this book ranges over the postapostolic biblical deposit. Brown is largely sympathetic to the Pastor's attempt to further the apostle's thought for believers standing in the Pauline tradition and to legitimate structures of church governance in the face of forces which would otherwise hasten the disintegration of the church.

Countryman, L. William. 1980. *The Rich Christian in the Church of the Early Empire: Contradictions and Accommodations.* New York/Toronto: Edwin Mellen Press. An enterprising study of attitudes toward wealth in the early church, the Pastorals included. Countryman argues that the benefaction culture of Greco-Roman urban society presented difficulties in the church since wealthy believers seem to have expected to play a role in the church analogous to that which they played in the wider society or the club. The Pastor urges the wealthy householders to give alms generously but not to compete with those set aside to teach and preach in the congregation.

Dibelius, Martin, and Hans Conzelmann. 1972. *The Pastoral Epistles.* Philadelphia: Fortress. Dibelius and Conzelmann's commentary has been dated by the demonstration by a number of recent scholars that from the beginning the social standing of the early Pauline Christians, especially its leaders, was likely to have been more well-to-do than these commentators assumed. Furthermore, the concept of "bourgeois Christianity," which Dibelius and Conzelmann argued encapsulates the social vision of the believers, does not seem to do adequate justice to the countercultural teaching of much of the letters, especially with respect to wealth. Nevertheless, the commentary is a valuable resource of illustrative material from the Greco-Roman era.

Donelson, Lewis R. 1986. *Pseudepigraphy and Ethical Argument in the Pastoral Epistles.* HUT 22. Tübingen: Mohr (Siebeck). One of the most important books to appear on the Pastorals in the last generation. Donelson argues that the pseudonymous author of the letters wrote to claim ownership of Paul in the face of heterodox interpretations of the apostle. The bulk of the monograph is devoted to an analysis of the Pastor's use of the technique of the rhetorical syllogism (enthymeme) in constructing his exhortations to his addressees. Donelson concludes with some telling observations about the theological and ethical distinctives of the author based on the logic of his exhortation.

Fiore, Benjamin. 1986. *The Function of Personal Example in the Socratic and Pastoral Epistles.* AnBib 105. Rome. Biblical Institute. A thorough examination of the rhetorically forceful use of positive and negative paradigms in the Socratic and Pastoral Epistles. An important discussion of the function of the personalia of both corpora.

Harding, Mark. 1998. *Tradition and Rhetoric in the Pastoral Epistles.* StudBL 3. New York: Peter Lang. An analysis of the interplay of Pauline tradition and Greco-Roman rhetoric in the Pastorals, the Pastor commending his interpretation of the Pauline deposit by the use of rhetorical strategies of argumentation.

Johnson, Luke Timothy. 1996. *Letters to Paul's Delegates: 1 Timothy, 2 Timothy, Titus.* Valley Forge, Penn.: Trinity Press International. A recent commentary arguing for the probable authenticity of the three letters. This work is part of a series in which the social and literary context of New Testament texts is elucidated as of first importance. As a result, Johnson has produced a commentary that is an excellent and readable resource of the Greco-Roman background of the Pastorals.

Judge, Edwin A. 1960. *The Social Pattern of Christian Groups in the First Century: Some Prolegomena to the Study of New Testament Ideas of Social Obligation.* London: Tyndale. An excellent introduction to the social world in which the Pauline mission was conducted. This seminal monograph has been highly influential in re-igniting scholarly interest in the social description of the churches of the New Testament era and the social setting of the Pauline mission.

Kidd, Reggie M. 1990. *Wealth and Beneficence in the Pastoral Epistles.* SBLDS 122. Atlanta: Scholars Press. A well-researched monograph critical of Dibelius and Conzelmann's "bourgeois Christianity" theory as applied to the moral vision of the addressees of the Pastorals. The great value of the monograph is Kidd's understanding of the benefaction culture of the letters. He shows that the wealthy members of the churches, now addressed as potential "overseers," were expected to set aside certain cultural expectations of honor and status associated with wealth and become generous benefactors of the congregations without expecting earthly rewards.

MacDonald, Dennis R. 1983. *The Legend and the Apostle: The Battle for Paul in Story and Canon.* Philadelphia: Westminster. MacDonald advances the contentious thesis that the *Acts of Paul* (*and Thecla*) preserves aspects of Pauline tradition in which the apostle was remembered as a countercultural preacher who valued the contribution of women in his mission and his churches. MacDonald argues that the Pastorals were written to silence story-telling women who kept this memory of Paul alive.

MacDonald, Margaret Y. 1988. *The Pauline Churches: A Socio-Historical Study of Institutionalization in the Pauline and Deutero-Pauline Writings.* SNTSMS 60. Cambridge: Cambridge University Press. Based on modern sociological models, MacDonald analyzes the process of the progressive institutionalization of the Pauline corpus from the era of community-building (the undisputed letters) to community-stabilization (Ephesians and Colossians) and to community-protection (the Pastorals). The author of the Pastorals is seeking to protect community life from the destabilizing effects of the false teachers.

Malherbe, Abraham J. 1987. *Paul and the Thessalonians: The Philosophic Tradition of Pastoral Care.* Philadelphia: Fortress. This is a significant book for understanding the pastoral thrust of the ministry of the historical Paul as it can be perceived in 1 Thessalonians. The Pastor sought to actualize this tradition about Paul in the Pastorals.

Martin, Seán Charles. 1997. *Pauli Testamentum: 2 Timothy and the Last Words of Moses.* Rome: Gregorian University. This monograph is a bold analysis of the relationship between the portrait of Moses and his adversaries in scripture and tradition and the portrait of Paul and the false teachers drawn by the Pastor. Martin is particularly compelling in his analysis of the testamentary features of 2 Timothy.

Meade, David G. 1986. *Pseudonymity and Canon.* WUNT 39. Tübingen: Mohr (Siebeck). An analysis of the relationship between pseudonymity and tradition in the Hebrew Bible and the literature of early Judaism and Christianity. Meade argues that pseudonymous attribution is a device intended as an assertion not of literary origins but of the claim to actualize authoritative tradition associated with the putative author.

Miller, James D. 1997. *The Pastoral Letters as Composite Documents.* SNTSMS 93. Cambridge: Cambridge University Press. Building on the earlier work of P. N. Harrison, Miller argues that the Pastorals are a disparate, archival anthology of authentic Pauline fragments supplemented over the course of a century by paraenetic materials formulated by a Pauline disciples committed to training and forming pastors after the Pauline model.

Quinn, Jerome D. 1990. *The Letter to Titus.* New York: Doubleday. Quinn died in the final stages of the writing of this large-scale work, which was to be followed by a commentary on 1 and 2 Timothy. Quinn argues that Titus was the first of the Pastorals to be written. The commentary is characterized by full notes on the Greek text together with discussions of the theology and social context of the letter.

Towner, Philip H. 1989. *The Goal of Our Instruction.* JSNTSup 34. Sheffield: JSOT Press. A thorough exegetical study of the paraenesis directed to the various groups that constitute the churches of the Pastorals. Towner is particularly critical of Martin Dibelius' "bourgeois Christianity" theory. He argues that the goal of the ethics of the letters is to promote the mission of the church. The letters do not prescribe an accommodation to the values of Greco-Roman society.

Verner, David C. 1983. *The Household of God: The Social World of the Pastoral Epistles*. SBLDS 71. Chico, Cal.: Scholars Press. A comparatively early foray into the social background of the Pastorals with respect to the Greco-Roman institution of the household. Verner elucidates the Pastor's indebtedness to the hierarchical conventional wisdom encapsulated in the letters.

Index

143

Other Books in This Series

What are they saying about the Ministerial Priesthood?
by Rev. Daniel Donovan
What are they saying about the Social Setting
of the New Testament?
by Carolyn Osiek
What are they saying about Scripture and Ethics?
(Revised and Expanded Ed.)
by William C. Spohn
What are they saying about Unbelief?
by Michael Paul Gallagher, S.J.
What are they saying about Masculine Spirituality?
by David James
What are they saying about Environmental Ethics?
by Pamela Smith
What are they saying about the Formation of Pauline Churches?
by Richard S. Ascough
What are they saying about the Trinity?
by Anne Hunt
What are they saying about the Formation of Israel?
by John J. McDermott
What are they saying about the Parables?
by David Gowler
What are they saying about Theological Reflection?
by Robert L. Kinast
What are they saying about Paul and the Law?
by Veronica Koperski